THE DRAMA RECIPE BOOK

The Drama Recipe Book

**ALAN MACDONALD &
STEVE STICKLEY**

MINSTREL

Eastbourne

Biblical quotations are from the
New International Version
© International Bible Society 1973, 1978, 1984
Published by Hodder and Stoughton

Cover design by W James Hammond

British Library Cataloguing in Publication Data

McDonald, Alan
    Drama recipe book.
    1. Christian life.—Dramatisations
    I. Title   II. Stickley, Steve

    ISBN 1-85424-075-7

Printed in Great Britain for
Minstrel, an imprint of Monarch Publications Ltd
1 St Anne's Road, Eastbourne, E Sussex BN21 3UN by
Cox & Wyman Ltd, Reading, Berks.
Typeset by Nuprint Ltd, Harpenden, Herts AL5 4SE

Contents

Dedication

To Sally and Janet,
two lovely wives who provide continual support
and encouragement
in so many forms, including culinary ones.

Acknowledgements

Our many thanks to the following people for their varied roles in helping to produce these unusual recipes:

The nimble fingers of Maggie Birchall, Sue Elkins, Michèle Taylor and Ingrid Wagner and their various typewriters, word processors, quills, etc; Trevor and Margaret Cooling at Stapleford House Education Centre for allowing the participatory ideas to be tried out on unsuspecting teachers; Paul Oakley and the children of Kids' Workshop at St Nicholas Church, Nottingham; Val Ogden for advice; and finally Katharine Key, David Purveur, Trevor Warlow, Meg Frost and Glyn Fussell for suffering some of the scripts in this book in their formative stages.

Performing Licence

A licence fee for an amateur group to perform all or some of the sketches in this book costs £15.00 for a period of five years. This includes all types of performance, ie on the street, church services, schools or public halls, regardless of whether admission is charged. Suitable acknowledgement should be made to Footprints Theatre Company wherever practicable. All rights are reserved, and the text may not be reproduced in any form. The material contained herein is for live theatre performances only; the sketches may not be recorded on to sound cassette, radio, video, television or film without prior permission in writing from Footprints Trust.

No performance of any kind may be undertaken without the licence.

Details of material requiring the licence may be found in the key on page 13. Workshops, meditations, stories, etc do not come under the terms of this licence and may be used freely.

A stamped, addressed envelope should be sent to: The Administrator (Licences), Footprints Theatre Company, St Nicholas' Centre, Maid Marian Way, Nottingham, NG1 6AE.

Note: all monies received will enable Footprints Trust to continue its work for schoolchildren.

Bonjour my little profiteroles!

'Ow is a chef like a minister, a teacher or a budding acteur? Because 'e is always 'ungry for ze new ideas of course.

'Ere is a recipe book simply oozing with ze water-mouthing dishes for all ages and occasions.

Inside you will find sweet and savoury scripts, pressure cooking workshops, jungle jelly children's stories, mulled wine meditations and fresh bread baked for Bible studies.

All you 'ave to do is say your grace, open up zis book and find ze recipe zat most, 'ow you say, pays ze bill for what you 'ave in mind.

To make it easy each chapter 'as suggestions for 'oo may find it deliciously appetising.

Enough! I can see your palate is wetting.

Bon Appetit!

Les Cargo

Key to Symbols and Abbreviations

The symbols at the head of each section are intended as an easy reference guide to suggested uses of the scripts and ideas in this book.

 Suitable for performance by a drama group or useful in development

 Can be performed by one or two people

 Suitable for performance in a church service

 Outreach

 Bible study

 Street theatre

 Workshop

 Suitable for schools

 For young children

 For youth groups

 Licence needed

Abbreviations of Stage Directions

CS	Centre stage	OSL	Offstage left
DS	Downstage	OSR	Offstage right
DSC	Downstage centre	SL	Stage left
DSL	Downstage left	SR	Stage right
DSR	Downstage right	US	Upstage
MSL	Midstage left	USC	Upstage centre
MSR	Midstage right	USL	Upstage left
OS	Offstage	USR	Upstage right

À LA CARTE

STARTERS

1. A pleasant appetiser?

Drama and Evangelism

Jesus once described himself as 'the bread of life'. Significantly he didn't liken himself to a sugary sweet, a stodgy pudding or a fizzy drink (Jesus was always controversial, but never anachronistic!); he talked about bread, a staple diet for life.

Despite our new-found consciousness of healthy eating, the sad fact is that relatively few people in our generation seem to be seriously searching for bread. Even if they are searching, apparently they are not finding, since the church in Britain is not growing significantly in numbers.

People must be attracted to its doors. Therefore, the argument runs, what we need are effective appetisers to stimulate people's awareness of their hunger.

Music has always been a powerful appetiser in this respect and has drawn many to their first experience of Christian teaching. The last decade, however, has seen a popular new addition to the menu: drama.

Drama has brought colour, life and humour into the church. It is capable of stopping pedestrians in the street, holding a class of schoolchildren spellbound and even breaking down the reserve of a congregation. Such effectiveness has not been lost on Christians; in a short space of time professional and amateur groups have flourished all over Britain. Drama has become the new appetiser for evangelism.

All of which should be very pleasing to Christians who have been ploughing a lonely furrow in theatre for many years. You might expect those writing books which offer ideas and scripts to be doubly pleased!

This book, however, begins with a chapter of warning for those who may be sincerely seeking to use its contents for the purpose of evangelism. If you're already tempted to skip these pages and get straight on to the scripts, then the danger we wish to avoid is looming large ahead.

To see how this danger has arisen, we must take a look at the stormy relationship between the church and drama in past history.

Drama, of course, is not a complete newcomer to the church. In medieval Britain, it had its origins in Latin liturgical plays that were acted out in church as an integral part of the service as early as the tenth century. These eventually gave way to the mystery or miracle plays which were performed in common English and taken out into the market place for all to enjoy. It was to be a long wait before drama was allowed back inside the doors of Mother Church again.

Theatre in the following centuries became the province of the world outside, and before too long found itself denounced by clergy as a haven for all kinds of vice, depravity and indecency. The Rev Jeremy Collier in 1698 spoke for many churchmen in his *Short View of the Immorality and Profaneness of the English Stage*.

By the eighteenth century the church was retreating from other areas of life. The Age of Reason exalted science, philosophy and rationalism, creating a humanistic world where religion had no influence. The church's response was to put a protective wall around those things that were 'spiritual', ie things such as prayer, worship, evangelism and acts of Christian charity. Two separate worlds were created, the secular and religious.

This legacy is still with us today. We talk easily of the difference between Christian and secular, and accept that the church has little or no influence in the areas of science, economics, politics, philosophy or the arts. If we return to the Bible, we find a Creator who is the God of all of life, yet we have reduced him to reigning over a narrow kingdom called 'spiritual activities'.

There are signs in our century of the retreat being reversed, and one of these is the acceptance of drama back into the church after centuries in the wilderness.

But before we become complacent we must ask why drama has had the hand of friendship extended to it again. Wary of the theatre's habitual preoccupation with sexual and violent themes, we have been anxious to have proof of drama's spiritual intentions before it can be allowed back in the door. In effect, drama has been charged an admission fee and the price demanded has been its service to evangelism.

We are entering controversial territory and before any reader becomes indignant, it is important to stress that there is nothing wrong with drama having an evangelistic effect. If a man finds faith through watching a play, no Christian can do other than praise the mystery of God's grace.

The danger we are seeking to point out is that if anyone comes to drama merely for its evangelistic potential, the results are likely to be disastrous.

Consider somebody attempting to write a sketch whose overriding aim is to put over an evangelistic message. When he comes to write a line of dialogue, he is not asking, 'What words are true and realistic for this character to speak at this point?', but rather, 'What words will communicate the message best?'

When he arrives at the end of his sketch, he cannot be ruled by the ending which would be most fitting and believable to the situation he has created; he must

Getting the message over

rather supply a punchline that leave his audience in no doubt about what the message of the sketch was.

The result of this approach is to produce drama that is compromised and insincere. It will quite probably make dull entertainment too, as all actions are marching towards an inevitable, predetermined end. Such writing is more worthy of the term 'propaganda' than theatre.

The medieval mystery plays were not created as the means to an end, of winning souls, but were meaningful and an end in themselves; a joyous celebration of the Biblical pageant of history from Creation to Judgement.

Our insistence on drama having an evangelistic function is rather like standing in a forest before a beautiful oak tree and exclaiming, 'What beautiful firewood!' An oak tree may well make good firewood, but its Creator made it to have a meaning in itself, as a thing of beauty to be enjoyed for its own sake. In the same way, drama has its own value as a gift from God to men: it does not have to be given a spiritual justification.

The eighteenth century's distinction between secular and spiritual has left us with split vision, so that we are forced to justify art when we bring it inside the Christian perimeter. In fact, the only thing that can be called truly Christian is a person who has received Christ— and therefore all his actions which are not sinful are equally spiritual. There is no distinction, for the Christian, between playing tennis or praying or acting in a play, 'For everything God created is good, and nothing is to be rejected if it is received with thanksgiving' (1 Tim 4:4).

This has widespread implications and not least for the Christian approaching drama. Firstly, there are no 'Christian' subjects, just as there are no secular ones. The person who writes a play about the life of Christ is not necessarily doing something more worthy than someone who writes about the breakdown of a marriage. Since God is the God of life who calls us to be salt for the whole earth, a Christian voice needs to be heard on politics, abortion, homelessness, unemployment, in fact anything that concerns mankind. The evangelistic truths of the gospel do not represent the limit of our horizons for involvement in theatre.

That is not to say, of course, that we should studiously avoid all mention of God, Jesus, and the cross. As someone has pointed out, it would be strange indeed if you visited an exhibition of Communist painting and found not one portrait of Marx. Our beliefs as Christians are central to our viewpoint and will naturally come through in our work, but the emphasis must be on *naturally*. If we begin with the overriding intention of putting over our message, then we will distort drama into nothing more than a vehicle. Nigel Forde of Riding Lights has expressed the consequences succinctly. 'What a shameful thing it would be for the greatest philosophy in the world always to produce art more closely related to the television advert than the works of Shakespeare.' (Nigel Forde *Theatrecraft*, MARC Europe.)

The second implication of abandoning all spiritual justifying of drama is one of the reasons for this book; it frees us to explore the subject in all its diversity. Drama in the church up to now has largely been translated as evangelistic sketches done by young people. The poverty of this definition is robbing us of immense riches. In the following pages, you will find examples of drama as storytelling, role-play, Bible study, games, worship, workshops and meditation, as well as a variety of sketches to be performed in different contexts by different age groups. Just as an oak tree has many branches, drama has many forms and unexplored pleasures. Let's not restrict ourselves to chopping firewood all the time!

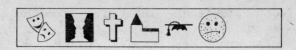

2. In the Soup

Thought for the Day
by Alan MacDonald

*People often ask for drama that can be performed by a single
person as they have to give a talk at a school assembly, an
evangelistic meeting or some other occasion. This piece
could be performed by a man or a woman (simply change
the name and the mention of the spouse) and needs no other
props than a sheaf of notes and, if possible, a microphone
on a stand. It relies on the actor capturing the soothing tone
of Radio Four's* Thought for the Day, *which should be
contrasted with the speaker's natural and irritable tones in
speaking to his son. It is vital to allow pauses for the little
boy's interruptions, as you would in a telephone
conversation with an imaginary person.*

ANNOUNCER: And now it's time for *Thought for the
Day* and today it comes from the Reverend Vernon Spore of St Jude's, Greater
Bunkham.
[*The actor assumes a pair of glasses to
denote the Reverend, and reads from his
notes.*]

REVD SPORE: Good morning. We live in a world of
change. Governments come and go,

prices are rising all the time, scientists are making new discoveries every day. Wherever I go I hear people saying...
[*He turns to his right abruptly, shouting.*] Justin, will you leave that microphone alone! I beg your pardon. [*He has lost his place.*] A world of change, er, where prices come and go, discoveries are rising all the time, and scientists are making new governments every day. But wherever I go I hear people saying... Take it out of your mouth, will you! Yes. Come here. I'm most dreadfully sorry. This is my son, Justin. His mother thought he'd be interested to see the inside of a radio studio [*With a trace of bitterness*] while she went shopping. He's only five, aren't you, Justin? Five and three days, yes. Now stand quietly while I talk to the people. Wherever I go I hear people saying...No, I know you can't see them, that's because I'm on the radio. [*Looking down at his feet*] No, not standing on it, I'm on it in the sense that I speak into this microphone here and thousands of people can hear me. Wherever I go I hear people saying, 'Is there anything today that hasn't changed?'

What? No, I wasn't alluding to your underpants, Justin. Yes, the blue and white striped ones look fine. Don't take them off, no, please don't...don't take them...oh well, thank goodness it's not television.

'Is there anything today that hasn't changed?' they ask, and my reply is... Well, you'll have to wait, won't you?

You should have gone before we came out. I'm sorry. My reply is, 'Friend, there is something today which doesn't change and that something is the certainty that God listens to prayer.'

Sometimes my companion will laugh, 'Ha! Ha!' and say, 'Prayer? You don't expect me to believe in that load of old...twaddle,' or words to that effect. To which I respond, 'Friend, that load of old twaddle happens to be twaddle I make a habit of everyday.'

'But prayer is mere fantasy,' objects my companion, 'how can you believe in a God that nobody has ever seen?'

'Ah,' I reply, 'Ah!' [Looking around the studio worriedly] Ahh...Justin? Justin! Come away from that desk immediately. The man doesn't want you touching those dials. Because he's quite capable of twiddling them himself. Now look, you've trodden on his turntable. Say sorry, then. Right, now perhaps I can finish speaking.

'Ah,' I reply, 'Nobody has ever seen God, but I, myself, have talked to him.'

No, Daddy's not talking to him now, he's talking to the people he told you about. Not invisible aliens, just ordinary people who have radio sets in their houses. Well, my voice goes through this microphone and into a, er...box, then it rides on the sound waves through the air and into people's radios. [Pause] Get up from the floor and stop giggling, Justin.

'Now, because we cannot...'

Yes, I said sound waves, Justin. Stop

22

that! You can't jump them because you can't see this kind of wave. Yes, they're here now. Well, all around us. It's no good trying to catch them in your trousers either. We don't need to take any home because they're already there. They're everywhere. Invisible but always present. You can believe what you like, Justin. Grown-ups know it's true. It is. Is! Is! Is! Is! Is! Of course, listeners, the fact that we cannot see God is no more a problem than... [*Looking in the direction of the presenter*] What do you mean, my time's up? I'm only half-way through. But I haven't got to the point yet. [*Crestfallen*] Oh.

Come on, Justin, it seems the man wants to play his records again. You haven't, have you? Where? [*He looks towards the control room, aghast.*] I think perhaps it's time that you and I made ourselves invisible. [*He backs away nonchalantly, then turns and runs.*]

3. Pâté Cake

Games

> *'The persistence of games is remarkable.*
> *Empires and institutions may disappear,*
> *but games survive...'*
> Roger Caillois, Man, Play and Games

Games are often regarded as the property of children, apart from when adults legitimise them by all the paraphernalia that accords them the status of sport.

If you have ever watched adults involved in a party game, however, you'll have noticed many of the characteristics normally associated with children's play: the release of laughter, shouting, energy and the relaxing of inhibitions. Games have the potential to take our attention away from ourselves and focus it upon the sheer enjoyment of an activity. In so doing, we are more able to 'be ourselves' and a sense of belonging in a group can be quickly fostered.

Rather than despising games as childish, anyone with an interest in drama or relationship-building in any context should collect games and develop their own variations. Here are a few we have found to be favourites with most age groups.

Silence and concentration games

Grandma's Footsteps

'Grandma' stands at one end of the room with her back to the other players, who stand in a line across the other end. Their object is to get near enough to touch her without being seen to move. The player who is Grandma turns round at intervals and the other players freeze in position: if any of them are seen moving they are called by name and sent back to the start line. The player who reaches Grandma first takes over the position in the next game.

An interesting variation is to play the game with Grandma standing in the middle of a circle of the other players.

Keeper of the Keys

This game demands complete silence. The keeper of the keys is blindfolded and sits in the middle of the room with the keys placed near him. The other players are seated around him in a circle about five yards away. The player in charge now points to another player in the circle and says 'Go'. This player becomes the thief and his object is to creep up, steal the keys and get them back to his place in the circle. The blindfolded keeper can prevent him by pointing in his direction. He has three chances to do this once the game has started; if he points exactly at the thief, the thief is out and must retire to his place. If the thief gets the keys back to his place, or the keeper exhausts the three chances without pointing to the right spot, then the thief is successful and becomes blindfolded as keeper for the next game. Other players in the circle must take care not to make noises that will distract the person in the middle.

'Adults relax their inhibitions
in games'

Story Games

Group Storytelling

This is a simple storytelling method which can lead to many variations. The organiser asks players to sit together in groups of three and number themselves one, two and three. He then gives them the first sentences of a story. '"Be careful!" said the old lady, "you nearly knocked me over." She picked up her shopping bag and...'

A number is then called out: if it is number two, all the twos must carry on the story from the word 'and', inventing any developments and characters they like. After about thirty seconds, the organiser calls another number and that person must continue the story, exactly where the number twos had broken off. After several minutes of this and some increase in the pace at which the story changes hands, the organiser says, 'Number threes finish off the story as fast as you can.'

The Dream Game

The safety of a group helps anyone to tell a story in the previous game. This one enables an individual to tell a story often with surprising results.

Send one or a few people out of the room. Then brief those left. You are going to pretend to have shared the same dream. The person you have sent out must try and find out what happened in the dream by asking questions with a 'yes' or 'no' answer. In fact, all the group does is to answer in the sequence 'yes, yes, no' to all the questions that are put.

The player is brought back into the room and the aim of the game is explained to them. At first they will think the task of discovering the dream impossible, but if encouraged to ask, the 'yes' answer usually helps them to proceed. The group can feign amazement at the questions that get a positive answer and vary their intonation of 'yes' and 'no' to disguise the sequence.

27

The player can be encouraged to continue discovering the exact details of the dream, until you judge the possibilities (or their patience!) to be exhausted.

If you have sent out several players they can be brought in one by one to play the game with different results. Intelligent people have been known to invent the most imaginative or bizarre stories, in the simple belief that the ideas are not their own!

Improvisation Games
(These are particularly suitable for moving into drama.)

Thank you

Players work in pairs, A and B. A must adopt some pose, say with one hand on one hip, and B then responds to this in some way, perhaps by putting his head under A's arm, as if he is a headless ghost. A says 'Thank you' and B must then strike up a pose. A responds to B's pose and B says 'Thank you'. The game can continue in this way for several minutes. Pairs should be encouraged to work instinctively and without pauses for thought.

Continuous Drama

A good game for improving group co-operation. Any number can be involved but a maximum of three are allowed to act at any time. The aim is to improvise a series of short dramas in recognisable styles, changing the style each time a new person joins the scene. For example, three people may begin with a scene from a Western. When this has run for a little while any player watching can step into the action and change it by introducing a new style by saying, for example, 'Nobody is to leave the room, a murder has been committed' thus setting up a 'whodunnit' genre.

The challenge for the actors is to guess the new style immediately and adapt their characters to fit in with it. There are now four players involved so to comply with the rules, one actor must find a natural way of leaving the scene. Again the scene progresses until a new player chooses to introduce another style such as opera, silent movie, sci-fi, romance, pantomime or any other.

It may help groups new to the game to establish a running order for joining in so that the drama continues without any confusion. Once you are familiar with the rules it is possible to allow the drama to flow spontaneously as any player wishes to join in.

VEGETABLES

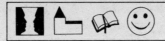

4. Hot Potatoes

The Moon in the Pool
by Alan MacDonald

*Storytelling is usually reserved for a children's audience,
but the power of a good story, well told, has equal effect on
adults, as anyone who has done the children's talk in a
service will know. Often a story will be remembered years
after the sermon has been forgotten. Here is a story to be
told to adults, in a service, Bible study, or any situation
where the unity of the Church is at issue.*

*Like any good parable, it can be enjoyed on two levels, so
children will also find it entertaining—and may well grasp
more of the meaning than many adults.*

*The effectiveness of the story depends on the narrator's
ability to supply the voices of the different animals. Each
animal should be given a distinct character voice, while the
narrator adopts the wide-eyed tones of fairy stories. The
story will work equally well with a male or female narrator.*

NARRATOR: Deep, deep in a dark forest, not far away
from where you live, there is a small clearing. In the middle of the clearing was
once a pool. Not a very deep pool—it
would only reach to your knees if you
paddled in it—and not very wide—you

32

could jump over it if you took a good run—but nevertheless, a pool.

It was five minutes to midnight. A million stars sparkled in the heavens and the full moon shone as brightly as anyone could remember.

There was a beat of wings and Septimus the owl alighted on the branch of an old elm.

'Five to twelve! Five to twelve!' he called.

For a moment everything was still; then, one by one, other animals began to emerge from the dark woods. Howard the donkey, Beatrice and Belinda the cows, Alf the eager beaver, a family of ducks called the Waddles, and a number of sheep who just liked to be called sheep.

'Well met by moonlight!' said Septimus, knowing that his apt quotation would be lost on most of the animals.

'Let's get started, then, there isn't much time,' moaned Howard the donkey.

Beatrice and Belinda objected. 'We're not all here. Where's Harriet?' There was a rustle of twigs and Harriet the goat, who had discovered some wild blackberries, joined the circle of animals.

'Pray proceed. I'm all ears, dears.'

Septimus drew himself up to his full ten inches. 'Brothers and sisters in the moon. As you know, we are met here tonight because we have faith that in a few minutes the Great Silver Face will descend from the sky and come to dwell for a short time in this, our humble forest pool...'

'Don't drag it out, Septimus,' complained Howard, 'we're here to decide what form the ceremony should take, not to listen to you twit-twooing on.'

'I was just about to state my proposal, if you'd show some patience, Brother Howard.'

'Well, what is it?' mooed Beatrice and Belinda.

'As you know, the Great Silver Face is something infinitely beyond our comprehension as mere beasts of the field. So I propose that if she appears in our pool we use the time to contemplate her beauty and purity.'

'In other words, do nothing,' said Howard gloomily.

'Meditation lifts the soul heavenwards,' argued Septimus, 'it is not nothing.'

At this point a new voice interrupted. 'Well, I agree with Howard,' said Alf the eager beaver. 'If the moon comes to swim in our pool we must do something for her. She'll want to see some response. I've drawn up some plans for building a roof over the pool and I'm prepared to start on the construction right now. What do you think?'

'Baah!'

'Well, the sheep agree,' said Septimus, 'but then they always do.'

Harriet the goat was unconvinced. 'What does the moon want with a wooden roof, Alf, dear heart? She's a free spirit, you can't trap her in a house. All she wants is our love, our adoration.'

'And how do we show that?' asked Howard.

'In song, of course, in song.' And

Harriet bleated a melody she had specially composed:

'O Moon you are so white,
You give us light,
You shine so bright...'

'Baah! Baah! Baah!' chorused the sheep, who loved to join in any song.

Howard was getting depressed. 'Now look what you've done. This is all getting rather sentimental and the moon could appear any moment now. I think what we need is something more solid. Now I know some good stories about the moon, so if you all listen you might learn something.'

'Quack! Quack! Quack! Quack!'

At this point there was an interruption from the Waddle family who had made their way down to the edge of the pool unnoticed. Father Waddle spoke up,

'Well, I'll tell you what we shall do. As soon as the moon appears we'll jump into it, immerse ourselves in it, bathe in its glory, so to speak.'

'Sacrilege! Out of the question! Shameful!' shouted everybody.

'It's obvious we'll never agree,' mooed Beatrice and Belinda. 'On the other side of the forest they say there's another pool where the moon sometimes appears. Belinda and I will go and worship in our own way.'

'No, no, no,' cried Septimus. 'Surely we can come to some agreement. This is disgraceful. Whatever will the Great Silver Face think of us?'

Nobody answered. They were all looking at the pool.

'Look. Oh wonder!' cried Harriet. 'There she is. The moon in the water!'

And before anyone could stop them the ducks had launched themselves forward with a great splash.

'Geronimo!'

Soon everyone was in the water, fighting and shouting at the tops of their voices.

'Oh moon you are so bright...Now listen, many years ago...Get out of there, you pagan ducks!...Help me get this roof up...Baah! Baah! Baah!'

[*a pause*]

When the last wave of the uproar had died away, the animals became aware of a terrible thing. The moon on the water had vanished.

5. Know yer Onions

Directing

Directors are a luxury that most Christians attempting drama assume they cannot afford. After all, you don't need someone to sit in a canvas chair and bellow 'Action' through a megaphone to begin practising a sketch for the Sunday service.

Why bother with a director? Similar questions are, why does an orchestra have a conductor? A house have an architect? A football team a manager? Because they would be a shambles of individual ideas otherwise, and sadly the same is often true of our drama, simply for want of a director.

You may object that you do not want to tackle full-length plays yet, your lighting design involves one fifty-watt bulb, the set consists of a table purloined from the vestry and the only prop is your mum's spider plant. You still need a director.

The reason is that, just like football teams and orchestras, actors, however inexperienced, need someone to help them work together. An outside eye is vital to look at the whole picture a piece of drama is giving. This is what the audience will see and it is no good one actor's rendition of Pilate's dilemma being spell-binding if he is standing right in front of Jesus all the time he's speaking.

Contrary to the popular idea, a director is not an egotist dictating to his actors, but a servant who is there to help them achieve the performance that most benefits the drama. Note: this may not be the performance that most benefits the actor.

Ideally the director should be someone who can best exercise the skills listed below. If there is no one available, you can use the person who is least involved in the drama to provide the director's 'outside eye' on this occasion.

Preparation

If the director's hat is handed to you, there is some work to be done before rehearsals. Firstly, if you have a script you must know it thoroughly and know how you envisage each part being played. This doesn't just mean knowing whether lines are spoken quietly or forcefully, but also what the actors are doing while they speak. A good method is to jot down suggested moves or actions in a column alongside the script. When it comes to rehearsals, your role is not to say, 'Now, John, you go to the window,' but to let the actor discover the most natural move himself, and have your suggestion ready if he needs it.

Secondly, consider if prayer, warm-up exercises, or games could be helpful before starting on your script. Few people can produce their best acting if they go into it 'cold'.

Thirdly, it is important to know what you aim to achieve in one rehearsal and how this fits into the time you have available before the performance. It may help to consider your rehearsal schedule in terms of three stages:

1. Blocking—working out roughly what happens in terms of movement.
2. Polishing—breaking the drama down into parts and paying attention to details.

3. Run-throughs—where you put the whole piece together.

What to look for

Acquiring the skills needed to direct well is about as simple as learning to play the violin. You can help your actors, however, if you at least know what you're looking for. Here are some of the most obvious areas a director must pay attention to:

1. Masking—are any of the actors obscuring each other from the audience when we need to see them?
2. Clarity—seems obvious, but can we hear and understand every word that is being spoken?
3. Motivation—have the actors thought out why their characters say or do a particular thing?
4. Characterisation—are the actors settling for easy stereotypes or developing believable identities? Try asking where their character lives, what he has on his toast, etc. You will soon find out!
5. Pace—when the whole piece is performed, are there unnecessary pauses that make it tedious, or is it played at such break-neck speed that the audience can't catch their breath?

Difficult Actors

If you try to direct you will soon discover you have some of these in your group. Some will feel you interfere too much, some that you say too little, some want to dominate performances while others are struggling to hide behind the furniture with embarrassment. There are no magic formulae for helping everybody. The director's skill is to discover if an individual responds best to encouragement or criticism, sympathy or discipline, and then to give it at the right moment. As a general guideline, though, criticism is a pill that can be swallowed best if a cup of encouragement is provided to wash it down.

6. Old Chestnuts

Second Hand Views
by Alan MacDonald

This is a versatile sketch which would work well in many situations, but particularly for an evangelistic occasion. It highlights the way many people have ready platitudes in answer to all life's problems. Even when it comes to the ultimate question of death, there is a general agreement to talk only in clichés and sayings that avoid having to face the reality of the event.

This piece exalts cliché to a high art form in the characters of Marge and Gloria who are the sort of middle-aged ladies who talk loudly on buses. It is essential that their gossip runs on at a relentless pace and is continually punctuated by 'mmm's', 'aah's' and 'oooh's'.

Richard and Antonio are young, bored hairdressers. Avoid the cliché of effeminacy, but the actors should take great care over their mimed hairdressing throughout the sketch.

Characters: MARGE, GLORIA—middle-aged ladies
                       RICHARD, ANTONIO—hairdressers

[*Two chairs side by side facing audience. Two towels over the back of them.* GLORIA *and* MARGE *are bent backward as if over washbasins.* RICHARD *and* ANTONIO *are washing their hair.* GLORIA *and* MARGE *give occasional murmurs of pleasure. Simultaneously* RICHARD *and* ANTONIO *lift the*

41

women back into an upright position and proceed to dry their hair vigorously. They stop. GLORIA *and* MARGE *turn to each other.*]

GLORIA: Marge!
MARGE: Gloria!
TOGETHER: Well, fancy!
[RICHARD *and* ANTONIO *raise their eyes to the heavens. They proceed to comb out the women's hair, all the while mimicking the women with their expressions.*]
GLORIA: Well, I must say, you're looking well.
MARGE: I can't complain, you know. Derek and the kids all right?
GLORIA: Oh, same as ever, we mustn't grumble.
MARGE: Mmm. Count your blessings.
GLORIA: Look on the bright side.
MARGE: Always a silver lining.
GLORIA: That's it, isn't it?
TOGETHER: As long as you're happy.
[RICHARD *and* ANTONIO *mouth the last comment. The women turn round to look at them suspiciously.*]
RICHARD: Your usual perm, Mrs Edwards?
ANTONIO: Your usual perm, Mrs Sharpe?
TOGETHER: If you would, Richard/Antonio. [*To each other*] Such nice boys.
[RICHARD *and* ANTONIO *proceed to put a few large curlers in their hair.*]
MARGE: Does Antonio always do your hair?
GLORIA: Ooh, I wouldn't be happy with anyone else. You get used to someone, don't you?
MARGE: Yes, I've always felt I can trust Richard. He's got such gentle hands. Ouch!
[RICHARD *has wound a curler too tight. He smiles winningly.*]
MARGE: So, how's life, Gloria? Keeping busy?
GLORIA: Oh, don't ask me, Marge.
MARGE: Really?

GLORIA:	Mmmm. It's better not to talk about it. [*Pause*] Well, if you must know, our Derek's mother died last week.
MARGE:	Oh, I am sorry. It must have been a shock for you, you poor love.
GLORIA:	Well, you never think it'll happen to *you*, do you?
MARGE:	No, but you can't go on living forever.
GLORIA:	And she had a good innings.
MARGE:	Mustn't grumble.
TOGETHER:	As long as you're happy.
RICHARD:	Have you got any perm lotion, Antonio?
ANTONIO:	I left it on the shelf. [RICHARD *goes upstage to look.*]
MARGE:	And you went to the funeral, did you?
RICHARD:	I wish you'd put the top back on.
GLORIA:	Well you have to, don't you?
MARGE:	Nice service?
ANTONIO:	[*putting in the last curler*] That all right, Mrs Sharpe?
GLORIA:	Mmmm. Beautiful.
MARGE:	Nice to have a good send-off.
GLORIA:	Oh, yes. A little cry never does you any harm and...
MARGE:	It might do you a bit of good, yes.
RICHARD:	Ready for the drier, Mrs Edwards?
ANTONIO:	Ready for the drier, Mrs Sharpe?
TOGETHER:	Put us under the microwave, boys. [*They giggle.*] [RICHARD *and* ANTONIO *turn their chairs round full circle and mime bringing the driers down. They exit, having given the women magazines.*]
GLORIA:	The vicar had such a lovely manner.
MARGE:	Mmmm. Well they have to, don't they, in their job? Lovely sermon?
GLORIA:	Oooh, I expect so. I can't say I listened,

	Marge. I will say, though, he came up to me special, and he says to me, 'I can't say how sorry I am, Mrs Sharpe.'
MARGE:	Ah, that's nice.
GLORIA:	'Well, no sense in crying over spilt milk, Vicar,' I says to him, I says, 'Worse things happen at sea. We just have to put these things behind us.'
MARGE:	Never a truer word spoken, Gloria.
GLORIA:	And you know what he says to me? As I live, he says, 'Well, death comes to all of us, Mrs Sharpe, and it's best to be prepared for it.'
MARGE:	Ooh, heavens above.
GLORIA:	Yes. 'There's no need to be morbid,' I says, 'Vicar.' There's some things it's better not to think too much about in this life—and death is one of them. Better to let well alone.
MARGE:	Take no thought for tomorrow.
GLORIA:	Let sleeping dogs lie.
TOGETHER:	As long as you're happy.

[*Re-enter* ANTONIO *and* RICHARD *unseen.*]

| ANTONIO: | [*loudly*] Time's up, ladies. |

[*Both women give a start and clutch at each other's hands.*]

MARGE:	Don't do that, Antonio.
GLORIA:	You'll be the death of me.
RICHARD:	We only want to take your curlers out.

[RICHARD *and* ANTONIO *start to do so.*]

GLORIA:	That's what they all say. [*Both women giggle.*]
	Yes, I said to him Marge, 'Vicar,' I said, 'You've only got one life...'
MARGE:	...so enjoy it while you can.
GLORIA:	Gather the rosebuds while you may.
MARGE:	Life life to the full.
GLORIA:	Make the most of it.

MARGE:	Tomorrow's another day.
RICHARD, ANTONIO:	...As long as you're happy.
MARGE, GLORIA:	Oh, you boys!

[RICHARD *and* ANTONIO *have taken out the curlers and show the women themselves in the mirror.*]

RICHARD:	All right, Mrs Edwards?
ANTONIO:	All right, Mrs Sharpe?
GLORIA:	What do you think, Marge?
MARGE:	What do you think, Gloria?
TOGETHER:	You don't look a day over thirty. [*they giggle and nudge each other. They get up from their seats, pay* RICHARD *and* ANTONIO, *and exit, still gossiping.* RICHARD *slumps in one of the chairs.* ANTONIO *begins to sweep up.*]
RICHARD:	They always depress me, those two.
ANTONIO:	Oh yeah?
RICHARD:	Yeah. Dyeing their grey hair blonde and behaving like schoolgirls.
ANTONIO:	Listen, the day people stop dyeing their hair, we're out of a job, right?
RICHARD:	Mmmm. [*Pause.* RICHARD *begins to sweep up.*] Antonio...
ANTONIO:	Yeah?
RICHARD:	What do you reckon happens when you die?
ANTONIO:	[*Incredulous*] I said *dyeing*, not *dying*! Tut!
RICHARD:	Yes, but the whole thing...You know, Heaven, God an' all that.
ANTONIO:	It's rubbish. Mumbo jumbo for old ladies.
RICHARD:	I don't know, maybe I'll look into it sometime.
ANTONIO:	You think too much, Richard. Look—as long as you're happy, eh? [*They freeze in their positions.*]

MAIN COURSE

7. Barbecued chicken

Street Theatre and its Problems

One of the most popular forms of theatre for Christians is street theatre. The precedent for taking drama out into the market place goes right back to medieval mystery plays, and out on the street is the one place we can be sure we're not preaching to the converted.

Unfortunately, street theatre is not the easiest style of performance to execute successfully. Picture the scene: Maureen, the youth leader, stands outside Marks and Spencer with a bucket of water. They are doing 'The woman at the well', and she is the woman. She launches into a long monologue about how unhappy she is. Nobody pays her much attention except a gentleman who interrupts to ask the way to the Post Office.

Kevin, dressed in rainbow braces (that mark him out unmistakably as Jesus) accosts her and asks for a drink. The manageress from Marks and Spencer asks if they would mind not blocking the doorway. Carrying the bucket, Kevin proceeds to tell Maureen all about herself, and she registeres great surprise, but her response is drowned out by a pneumatic drill nearby. Maureen resorts to hysterical melodrama and a small crowd does indeed gather to see if she needs help. Meanwhile a tramp is washing his face in the bucket. Kevin calculates

49

it is time to invite everyone to tonight's guest service, but just as he begins a policeman moves in, having noticed a disturbance...

You see the problems. Obviously this is an exaggerated description, but once you are out on the street, there is no guarantee of what you may have to cope with. Street theatre is a voyage into the unknown, but if we can learn from some of Kevin and Maureen's mistakes we will certainly fare better than they did.

1. *They didn't choose their site carefully.* A good street theatre site has enough room for a crowd to gather without blocking a public thoroughfare. If possible you should have your own nucleus of a crowd to stand defining the acting area at the outset.

2. *They didn't make it clear that this was a theatrical performance.* Passers-by will not feel safe to stop unless they are sure this is an organised spectacle. Bright, dramatic costumes will help, and music, mime or slapstick to draw a crowd will ensure you get an audience for the *beginning* of your drama.

3. *Their play relied on words.* Nowhere is it truer that action speaks louder than words than in the street. Distractions on all sides mean that your audience will be able to hear only the simplest of dialogue. The more the story is told by movement and gesture, the better. If you need words, they will carry better when they are sung or spoken in unison by more than one actor.

4. *They hadn't a clear point to communicate.* Simplicity again is the keynote. It is important to decide what you are aiming to achieve and have realistic objectives. What happens at the end of your street theatre, if anything? People will move away quickly if there is a pause, so your programme must run smoothly through to its conclusion.

5. *They assumed some knowledge of their subject.* The average man in the street is not familiar with the story of the woman at the well, or perhaps any part of the Bible except the Ten Commandments, seven of which

he can't remember. Make sure your drama doesn't take anything for granted. If God or Jesus are represented, that must be clear, and words like 'saved' or 'sin' must be given concrete reality by the drama.

6. *They didn't inform the police.* It is always wise to get police permission for any open-air event. It might not be a bad idea to warn the manageress of Marks and Spencer, either!

8. Barbecued burger

One Man Went to Sow
by Alan MacDonald

This street-theatre piece is a proven crowd-puller, since it employs actors dressed as morris-dancers, a familiar and appealing outdoor spectacle for many. The sung dialogue and strong action help to make it clear and visual.

Ideally you need three male actors with strong singing voices. Paying attention to costume with brightly coloured braces, garters with bells, etc will also pay dividends.

The stage directions included here are intended as guidelines, but you may wish to develop them yourselves in rehearsal. The main comedy relies on a slapping sequence in which SINGER TWO *nearly always comes off worse. The melody used is 'John Barleycorn', a traditional folk song.*

	[*They stand close together in a line with* TWO *in the middle.*]
ALL:	There came three men from out of the west With spades and rakes and hoes, And they have scattered many a seed To see if it will grow.
	(Chorus) Sing right foot first

52

And slap your knee
Left hand, right hand, slap!
[*All slap knees, clap,* ONE *and* TWO *clap hands together while* THREE *slaps* TWO *round the back of the head.*]

(Verse One)

ONE: [*sings*] Up stepped the first with a handful of seed
Which he threw upon the path
[ONE *hops forward scattering seeds, then back into line.*]

ALL: [*chant*] Trample, trample, stamp!
Trample, trample, stamp!
[*Trample left and right foot, stamp by jumping forward, both feet together.*]

ONE, THREE: Caw! Caw!
TWO: Gobble, gobble, munch!
ONE, THREE: Caw! Caw!
TWO: Gobble, gobble, munch!
[ONE *and* THREE *face out, flapping wings,* TWO *faces front, flapping and eating.*]

ONE: But what was left that wasn't squashed
[ONE *and* THREE *sit on* TWO'*s back.*]
The birds had for their lunch.

ALL: Peck, gulp!
[*Swallowing seed*]

(Chorus)
Sing right foot first
And slap upon your knee
Left hand, right hand, slap!
[*All slap knees, clap,* TWO *and* THREE *clap hands together while* ONE *slaps* TWO *round the back of the head.*]

(Verse Two)

THREE: [*sings*] Up stepped the next with a handful of seed
Which fell among the rocks

	[THREE *hops forward then back, scattering seed.*]
ONE, TWO:	[*speak*] Grow, grow
THREE:	Soak up the sun
ONE, TWO:	Grow, grow
THREE:	Soak up the sun

[*They grow like plants from crouching to standing.*]

Water! Water!

ONE, TWO:	Shrivel and waste
THREE:	Water, Water!
ONE, TWO:	Shrivel and waste.

[*They shrivel and die, leaning on top of each other with* THREE *at the top and* TWO *at the bottom.*]

THREE:	[*sings*] And all for the want of H_2O
	Those plants did dehydrate...

[*They groan and collapse on top of* TWO.]

TWO:	[*just audible*] Get off!

(Chorus)
Sing right foot first
And slap upon your knee
Left hand, right hand, slap!
[*All slap knees, clap,* ONE *and* TWO *clap hands together.* TWO *ducks when* THREE *goes to hit him round the head. He turns triumphantly to* THREE *until* ONE *hits him from behind,* THREE *providing the noise of the slap.*]

(Verse Three)

TWO:	[*sings*] Up stepped the last with a handful of seed
	Which he threw among some thorns

[TWO *steps forward then back, scattering seed.*]
[*speaks*] Grow, grow, soak up the sun

	[TWO *grows upward.*]
ONE, THREE:	Thorns, thorns, prickle and point
	[ONE *and* THREE *entwine their arms like thorns around* TWO's *legs.*]
TWO:	[*hopefully*] Grow, grow, soak up the sun?
ONE, THREE:	Choke, choke, throttle and croak
	[*The thorns grow up to his neck.*]
TWO:	[*sings*] But when the shoots those thorns did see
	They really felt quite choked...eurgh!
	[ONE *and* THREE *choke him backwards into the ground.*]

(Chorus)

[ONE *and* THREE *begin this alone, with* TWO *trying to rejoin the dance.*]

Sing right foot first
and slap upon your knee
Left hand, right hand, slap!

[*Slap knees, clap,* ONE *and* THREE *on the last slap both hit* TWO *in the face.* TWO *can provide the noise of the slap and, if desired, spit out broken Polo mints for teeth!*]

(Verse Four)

ONE:	[*sings*] At last the three took what was left
	And planted in good soil
	[ONE *hops forward and back, scattering seed.*]
ALL:	[*speak*] Grow, grow, give birth to more
	[*They grow like plants as before.*]
	Grow, grow, give birth to more.
	[*They pause, embarrassed, unsure of how to represent this. Ad lib comments, 'Give birth to more? Who's going to do that? You are!' etc.* TWO *is volunteered to improvise. He puts his finger in his cheek and makes a popping noise, followed by a baby's cries.*]
TWO:	Wah! Wah! Wah! Wah!

[ONE *and* THREE *push him forward so that he does a handstand with them supporting his legs. They slap his bottom together.*]

ONE, THREE: Slap!

TWO: Ow!

[*He is put down and sucks his thumb.*]

ONE: [*sings*] And they did reap a harvest ripe
Of many ears of corn
[*In rhythm*, ONE *and* THREE *stack bales of wheat.* TWO *leans on top of the pile.*]

(Chorus)
Sing right foot first
And slap upon your knee
Left hand, right hand, slap!
[*This time* TWO *succeeds in ducking low so that* ONE *and* THREE *slap each other's face.* TWO *provides the sound effect. While they are arguing over this he steps forward to address the audience.*]

TWO: There is another version of this traditional folk song which goes something like this:

ALL: [*Sing at double speed standing in their original line.*]
There came three men from out the west
Their names will not be new
They are Father, Son and Holy Ghost
Who offer life to you.

(Chorus)
Sing right foot first
And slap upon your knee
Left hand, right hand, slap!
[*All slap knees, clap and duck on the final beat, expecting to be hit. They look up and laugh sheepishly.*]

ONE: But some seed falls upon the path
[*Dances to one side, singing in the melody of*

56

	the opening verse line. TWO *and* THREE *lean casually on each other and say the following in rhythm.*]
THREE:	Jesus?
TWO:	You must be joking!
THREE:	Chortle, chortle
TWO:	Giggle, grin
THREE:	Nudge, nudge
TWO:	Wink, wink
TWO, THREE:	Look at him
	[*They point derisively at* ONE *who poses as a devout Christian.* ONE *rejoins the line and* THREE *moves to one side, singing.*]
THREE:	And some seed falls upon the rocks...
	[ONE *and* TWO *pose back to back at a party, holding drinks.*]
ONE:	Jesus?
TWO:	You've got to admire him, but...
ONE:	Drink up, drink up!
TWO:	Game of squash?
ONE:	BMW?
TWO:	Mine's a Porsche!
	[*They raise their glasses.* THREE *returns to line and* TWO *steps out to sing.*]
TWO:	[*sings*] And some are strangled by the thorns...
	[ONE *taps* THREE *on the shoulder as if he is a salesman making him an offer.*]
ONE:	Jesus?
THREE:	I'd love to...if only I had time.
	Worry, worry
ONE:	Take a pill
	[*Throws one into his open mouth.*]
	Six months credit
	[*Thrusts form into his stomach.*]
THREE:	Pays the bills.
	(Verse Five)
ALL:	[*return to line and sing.*]

And those three men from out the west
Looked sadly on the view
They are Father, Son and Holy Ghost
And still they speak to you.

(Chorus)
Sing shut your eyes
Put your fingers in your ears
Pretend that you can't hear.
[*They stand one behind the other*, TWO *in front*, ONE *covering* TWO's *eyes and* THREE *stopping his ears.*]

9. Sweet and Sour talk

The Family Harmony
by Alan MacDonald

This sketch has proved very popular with young and old alike, probably because it comes so near the truth. It could be suitable for a family service, or any occasion where the audience is predominantly Christian. The family is often the place where we let our true selves come out into the open and we cannot hide behind superficial spirituality. This sketch faces us with the truth that to 'love our neighbour' does not exclude those living in the same house as us.

Characters: FATHER, MOTHER, DAUGHTER, SON, VOICE OF PHOTOGRAPHER.

[*A family posed for a photograph.* MOTHER *and* FATHER *sit at the front.* DAUGHTER *and* SON *stand at the back. All are linked by physical expressions of togetherness.*]

PHOTOGRAPHER'S VOICE:	[*off*] Say 'Cheese' please.
ALL:	Cheese please. [*They smile and hold the expression.*]
FATHER:	We are a Christian family.
MOTHER:	A happy family.
DAUGHTER:	A loving family.
SON:	A caring family.

MOTHER:	God bless this house.
DAUGHTER:	Charity begins at home.
SON:	The family that prays together stays together.
FATHER:	Christ is the head of this household. We are a Christian family. We take God's Word as our guide.
MOTHER:	'Wives submit to your husbands as to the Lord.' [*Her husband turns to her, smiles and kisses her cheek, turns to front.*]
FATHER:	[*under his breath*] Except over money.
MOTHER:	What?
FATHER:	Nothing, nothing.
MOTHER:	No, what did you say?
FATHER:	It was a joke. It doesn't matter.
MOTHER:	'Except over money,' you said. You think I'm not submissive over money?
FATHER:	I didn't say that.
MOTHER:	Because I *needed* a winter coat. You're not going to pretend I didn't need one. If you expect your wife to shiver through the winter in the same old rag of a raincoat; if that's your idea of submissive, then it certainly isn't mine.
FATHER:	I just think with things the way they are, we might have discussed it.
MOTHER:	Because I don't think they had Arctic winters in the Apostle Paul's day, if you don't mind me saying. I don't think when he came up with this submissive line, he was expecting wives to submit to hypothermia.

FATHER: Let's drop it, shall we?
[*They smile thinly at each other. Everybody returns to their original smiling pose.*]

DAUGHTER: 'Children, obey your parents in everything.'
[DAUGHTER *exchanges loving looks with parents.*]

MOTHER: Including what time you come in, young lady.

DAUGHTER: Mother!

MOTHER: I know, I know, the party was just getting going when you left.

DAUGHTER: Well, it was. Tarquin couldn't believe I had to be home by midnight.

MOTHER: I hope you told him that while you're living at home, you do what your parents tell you.

DAUGHTER: No. [*Pause*] I told him Dad beats you if I'm not home on time.

MOTHER: Jennifer!

DAUGHTER: Well, honestly, Mum, we're not living in the dark ages any more. You've got to start accepting me as an adult. Haven't you, Dad?

FATHER: [*who hasn't been listening*] Mmm? Of course we do, darling.
[*They return to their poses again. FATHER puts a reconciliatory arm around his wife.*]
'Husbands, love your wives and do not be harsh with them.'
[*The wife immediately begins to mime driving a car. The other three are passengers and sway with the car's movement accordingly.*]

MOTHER: Huh!

FATHER:	What do you mean, 'Huh'? I'm very patient with you.
MOTHER:	When it's you driving, yes.
FATHER:	Slow down, slow down. [*He is putting his foot down.*]
MOTHER:	The footbrake's on my side, darling. Because you get so nervy, it makes me nervy.
FATHER:	[*hanging on to his seat*] I'm not nervy. That lorry's signalling... he's signalling. [*He continues telling her this while she talks.*]
MOTHER:	Don't be ridiculous. Look at you now, you're like a cat on hot bricks. Honestly! Why can't you relax? I have passed my test, actually, first time, which is more than some people did, and I've been driving eleven years without a serious accident, you'd think...[*She is looking at him.*]
FATHER:	[*urgently*] He's signalling! [*A screech of brakes. They all lurch forward.*] You stupid woman! Why don't you watch the road?
SON:	Don't shout at her, Dad.
FATHER:	Shut up! [*The MOTHER's face crumples. A slight freeze is held. Then they all return to their original pose positions.*]
SON:	'Honour your father and mother.' [*To audience*] That's pretty difficult, actually, isn't it? I mean, you've seen what they're like. Dad always shouting at Mum, Mum complaining about the way he treats her,

both of them nagging at us to do this, do that, tidy this, don't say that. It also says somewhere, 'Parents, do not exasperate your children.' They ought to take note of that. I'll tell you, when I have children, I'm not going to be like them.

[*His sister has been mimicking his snootiness. He turns, sees her and shouts.*] Shut up!

FATHER: [*soothing*] We are a Christian family. We take God's Word as our guide.

PHOTOGRAPHER'S
VOICE: [*off*] Say 'humility' please.

ALL: [*smiling as before*] Humility please!

PHOTOGRAPHER'S
VOICE: [*off*] Now let's have a natural one, shall we? Ready?

[*They all assume physical gestures of anger and aggression with each other.*]

That's super!

10. Stir-fry Special

A Youth Workshop

This workshop is designed for youth groups not necessarily accustomed to drama. Aims: to initiate constructive relationships and a creative environment in which to explore a parable from a new angle. Participants should be encouraged to wear soft shoes and clothes that are suitable for physical activity.

1.   Without warning or introduction get the group to play:

Kneecaps

Everyone grabs hold of their own kneecaps. The aim is to touch as many knees as possible without letting others grab your knees. Once you say 'go'—watch out! Latecomers can easily join in and this horse-play activity will help to loosen things up a little...to say the least.

(If you feel this is too threatening for an inhibited group then find a more sedentary game from 'Paté Cake', page 25.)

(5 minutes)

2.   Arrange the group into two lines facing each other, approximately one metre apart. Point out that this exercise is to help us understand how we take communication for granted. Explain that you want each to

describe to their partner the object that you are about to place in their hand. Emphasise that you should not give obvious clues such as 'something you wear on your wrist that tells the time'. Rather, encourage them to describe its weight, shape, texture, dimensions, type of material etc. Get them all to close their eyes and one line to put their hands behind their back. Into their hands place a small object eg egg-cup, corkscrew, scissors, a pipe, bicycle clips, toy car, etc. No one is to talk until you say 'go'. They open their eyes and those with an object start describing it while their partner simply listens—no interrogations permitted! Allow one minute only for them to explore the details of their own particular object. Stop the hubbub and move quickly down the middle of the line asking each listener what they think their respective partner's object may be. The results are often hilarious. Swop over and repeat with new objects to see if they can do any better.
(10 minutes)

3.   Sit the group in new sets of pairs. Give everyone thirty seconds to think of a situation they have found themselves in fairly recently; it could be something embarrassing, frightening, boring, humorous, intriguing, etc. Then each tells the other about the incident while their partner listens, each no longer than 2 minutes. Encourage them to relate details.

Manner of the word

Explain that this time they will retell the incident in the manner of the word you will show them, eg enthusiastically or shyly. Get one partner to close their eyes while you hold up a card with the word on. Allow only 1 minute for the tellers to relate the incident again in this new fashion and then get the listeners to guess what the word was. Repeat with a different word and swapping roles. (Obviously the tellers in each case must *not* use the word on the card!)
(15 minutes)

4. Bank Robbery

Still in the same pairs (or threes depending on numbers) get them to their feet to act out a simple bank robbery. The scenario is as follows:

a) Robber enters the bank.
b) Money is demanded from the cashier(s).
c) Something happens.
d) Robber exits.

Give each pair a card with a different adverb on, and the robbery should be carried out in the manner of this word so that the audience should be able to guess it. Words could include: gloomily, athletically, religiously, lazily, hesitantly, graciously, etc. Give each pair five minutes to devise and practise their scene. Watch each scene in turn, encouraging the audience to guess the word at the end. (We've never known this exercise to fail. It is great fun.)
(25–35 minutes)

5. Puzzling Parables

Read out a simplified version of The Lost Son (Luke 15:11–32), ideally expressed in your own words. Shuffle the cards used in the previous exercise while you tell the pairs to find another pair to form groups of four. Explain the plot in stages as for the bank robbery and get them to decide on their characters. They may need to play more than one part or to change the sexes of the characters.
(3 minutes)

Deal two cards to each group. These must be kept secret from other groups. Explain that any two characters must behave in the manner of these words and that it is up to them how they cope with this. The aim is for the audience to guess eventually which character is behaving in the manner of which word. Give them ten minutes to devise it. Watch each group, guessing at the end of each story. (It is a good idea to encourage them to set the drama in a context of their choice, eg modern

day in *Dallas* or *EastEnders*, or a Victorian melodrama, etc.)
(25–35 minutes)

6. Finish off with a brief discussion about difficulties in communication and what the story of the Lost Son communicates to us.
(5–10 minutes)

Robbing a bank religiously

11. Red Herrings

Bus-stop Theology
by Alan MacDonald

Originally written for a conference on Christian social action, this script is easy to perform and has a wide application. It could serve as a useful reminder that action speaks louder than words in any context where 'a Christian approach' is under discussion, eg a sermon, Bible study or conference.

Effective performance of the dialogue relies on the relationship between the two opposite characters. The girl needs to be a well dressed, keen young Christian who is caught between her desire to evangelise and her wariness of the opposite sex. The man is slightly older, lower class, but confident of his opinions and charm. He should be dressed in denims or similar and chews gum in the aggressive open-mouthed manner beloved of schoolboys.

[*A bus-stop stand.* GIRL *is waiting at it, reading a weighty Christian book. A* MAN *approaches and queues behind her. He is chewing gum. Pause.*]

MAN: Good book, luv?

GIRL: Pardon?

MAN: Good book is it? Yer reading. Thriller, is it?

GIRL: Er, not exactly. It's a Christian book, actually.

MAN: Oh.

GIRL: It attempts to reach some answers about some of the pressing issues in society today.

MAN: Oh yeah? Like 'What time's the number 34 coming?' That sort of thing?

GIRL: No, social issues. Like the bomb, poverty, abortion, marriage and divorce, unemployment; that sort of thing.

MAN: Oh. I'm unemployed.

GIRL: Are you?

MAN: Yeah. Laid off ten months ago. That's the government for you in'it? All these cutbacks.

GIRL: Is it? [*She flicks furiously through her book.*] But don't you agree...'The ultimate solution belongs to the realm of macro-economics. Everybody seems to be agreed that unemployment is due to the current world recession, and that it can be overcome only by more trade bringing more demand, bringing more jobs.'

MAN: Yep. [*Pause*] That's the government for you, in'it? The poor get poorer and the rich stuff their faces.

GIRL: [*to herself*] Poverty, poverty. [*Finds appropriate chapter.*] Yes, well...'All of us are shocked by the poverty of millions and disturbed by the injustices which cause it. Those of us who live in affluent circumstances accept our duty to develop a simple lifestyle, in order to contribute more generously to both relief and evangelism.'

MAN: 'Ave some chewing gum.

GIRL: Oh, thanks. No, I won't. I've just had breakfast. [*Pause*]

MAN: You married?

GIRL: [*edging away*] No, no...but I've got a boyfriend.

MAN: Well, take my advice. Don't marry him. Getting married is like stickin' yer 'ead in a gas oven. I should know. I done it three times.

GIRL: But, er...'Human sexuality is a divine creation and human marriage a divine ordinance.'

MAN: Yer, well, sex is all right, I'll give yer that.

GIRL: No, I mean, 'The marriage bond is more than a human contract, it is a divine yoke.'

MAN: After a while the yoke wears a bit thin, know what I mean?
[*He laughs.*]

GIRL: [*laughs uncertainly*] I suppose you're right.

MAN: No, the trouble is, women always want their own way, don't they? They want to be the ones wearing the trousers these days. That's what women's lib's done for us.

GIRL: Ah, feminism, you mean. [*Consults book.*] 'It is a woman's basic right and responsibility to discover herself, her identity and her vocation...

MAN: [*to someone going past*] Morning, allright?

GIRL: The fundamental question is in what relationship with men will women find and be themselves? Certainly not...

MAN: Oi, careful! Did you see that? He pulled right out in front of that woman on the bike and made her go off the road. [*Shouts*] You alright, luv? [*To* GIRL] Well, aren't you gonna help? 'Er shopping's gone all over the place.

GIRL: Oh, yes, of course. Help.
[MAN *exits speaking.*]

MAN: Yeah, I saw it, luv, pulled right out, didn't he?

GIRL: [*back in book*] Now, where is it?...Ah! 'Involvement: Is it our concern?'
[*She holds her pose, considering the dilemma.*]

12. Devilled Kidneys

A Tempting Offer
by Alan MacDonald

*Often a church does not lend itself well to staging drama,
but here's a piece where the building is an essential
backdrop to the action. Even if your church lacks
performance space at the front, the movement around the
body of the church means that the sketch can still be
successfully staged.*

*The theme here is the strength of the true church, which
is underlined by the Devil who knows what he is up
against. The effectiveness of the piece hinges on the subtle
portrayal of the Devil, not as a mythical figure with horns
and pointed tail, but as a plausible property shark. The
character might be dressed in a dark suit with a deep red
shirt and bow-tie. The audience should only suspect his
true identity as the dialogue unfolds. Mr Bligh, the estate
agent, is affable and eager to please. Both actors should be
aware that as they move around the church, good voice
projection is vital.*

*The stage directions here suppose a church with three
aisles, a door at the back and a chancel at the front. They
can obviously be adapted to the design of your church so
that the actors are seen as much as possible.*

Characters: MR BLIGH—an estate agent
              NICK—a property shark
              CHOIR

[*A small choir is holding hymn practice at the far end of the chancel. They are singing 'Jesus the name high over all' softly. The singing should continue as background until near the end of the sketch, as if they're practising it again and again.* MR BLIGH *the estate agent enters, waves awkwardly to the* CHOIR, *and looks around the church at the front (chancel) end.* NICK *enters by the back door and strides confidently up the centre aisle, carrying a briefcase which he sets down at the front of the chancel.*]

MR BLIGH: Morning! Are you the gentleman who 'phoned earlier?

NICK: That's right. [*Shaking hands*] Very pleased to meet you.

MR BLIGH: I'm afraid I didn't catch the name, Mr... er...

NICK: Nick. Please call me Nick.

MR BLIGH: Right you are, Nick. Shall we take a look around?
            [*He places a hand on his client's shoulder.* NICK *unexpectedly wheels round, causing him to remove the hand immediately.*]
            Good. I'm afraid the er...vicar said there might be something going on this evening, but he was quite happy for us to look round. [*Indicating the* CHOIR] Some sort of hymn practice. Still, we won't disturb them.

NICK: No, they're not to know who I am, are they?
            [*He laughs.*]

MR BLIGH: Mmm? Oh, they wouldn't mind, I'm sure. The place is up for sale, so naturally they can't object to prospective buyers viewing. I must say you're the first, though. Not much you can do with an old church these days, is there?

72

NICK:	Oh, yes, for my purposes, a great deal.
MR BLIGH:	[*surprised*] Oh! Well, I suppose with the necessary renovation—and will you redesign?
NICK:	Totally.
MR BLIGH:	Good, well let's show you round then.
NICK:	[*glaring at the* CHOIR] Are these people going to be long?
MR BLIGH:	No, no, I expect they'll draw stumps soon. [*He leads the way across the front and down the left-hand aisle.*] As you can see some of the stonework is in pretty bad shape, [*He pauses to knock on a wall.*] but that may not mean the foundations are faulty.
NICK:	The foundations are fine.
MR BLIGH:	How do you know?
NICK:	The place is built on rock. I checked. [*They move on to the back of the church.*]
MR BLIGH:	Oh, well, that means it should last a while yet then.
NICK:	Perhaps. [MR BLIGH *pauses at the back of the centre aisle to offer a cigarette.*]
MR BLIGH:	Do you smoke, Nick?
NICK:	Yes.
MR BLIGH:	[*looking at him and laughing nervously*] Oh, I see you already are. [*They continue up the centre aisle.*]
NICK:	When are they going to stop that singing?
MR BLIGH:	I'm afraid it's all in a bit of a state. The filth on these pillars for instance—everything in here will need a pretty thorough cleaning.
NICK:	[*still glaring at the* CHOIR] They look as if they've already had it.
MR BLIGH:	The pillars?
NICK:	No, I was referring to the body of the

73

church.

MR BLIGH: Quite...you've gone rather red. How are you feeling?

NICK: [*darkly*] Diabolical.

MR BLIGH: Oh dear. Well, be finished in a jiffy. [*He moves to the front of the right-hand aisle, looking up at the ceiling.*] As you can see, the main body's got quite a few serious cracks in it. There's been some plaster work over the years but of course the cracks re-appear if they're not attended to...

NICK: Don't be fooled, the structure's stronger than you think.

MR BLIGH: Sorry? Why do you say that?

NICK: [*impatiently*] Because I know the architect. This church has withstood hundreds of years of battering and all there is to show for it is a few tiny cracks. You'll have to wait for a major rift in the walls before you see some real crumbling. [*He shivers.*]

MR BLIGH: You don't look at all well. Are you cold?

NICK: I'm used to a somewhat warmer atmosphere.

MR BLIGH: If you buy I can recommend a firm to install modern heating...

NICK: [*returning to his briefcase where he left it*] I can provide my own, thank you. Now, let's get down to business. What did you say the property was priced at?

MR BLIGH: [*coming back to join him in the chancel*] Well, £215,000 was our original figure, but...

NICK: Agreed. I'll pay in cash, I have the money with me. [*He produces a roll of notes from the briefcase and gives them to MR BLIGH.*]

MR BLIGH: [*taken aback*] Right you are, then. We'll have to sign the contracts but we can do that at the office. I'll get in touch with the owner...

NICK: [*aghast*] The owner? He knows about the

	sale?
MR BLIGH:	Oh, yes. It's authorised by the Church Property Board.
NICK:	Of course, the Property Board.

[*The* CHOIR *come to an end of their singing at this moment.*]

MR BLIGH:	Yes, I'll give them a ring straight away. [*He starts to go.*] Are you coming, er...Nick?
NICK:	I'll just have a last look around. These people seem to have finished at last.
MR BLIGH:	I'll be in the car, then.

[*He sets off down the centre aisle but looks back half-way down.*]

As a matter of curiosity, what are your plans for the church? If you don't mind telling me, of course.

NICK:	Oh, it's not secret. I plan to demolish it. Reduce it to nothing.
MR BLIGH:	To demolish it? I see, and then what?
NICK:	Nothing.
MR BLIGH:	[*bemused*] Ah. Right you are. [*He goes on his way, exiting by the back door.* NICK *now turns with his back to the audience to greet the* CHOIR, *who, having packed up, are coming towards him.*]
NICK:	Good evening to you, friends. I've just been admiring your church. Allow me to introduce myself. I'm going to be the new owner. [*He laughs sinisterly. The* CHOIR *have stopped in their tracks. His laughter builds up, till he throws his head back and sends the sound echoing round the building like the laughter of hell.*]

13. Rabbit

Writing for Radio

You don't hear much drama on local radio. Why? Well, like a lot of things, there's normally not a budget for it, it's difficult and time-consuming to produce well, and it simply doesn't lend itself to inclusion in general programming schedules. The basic menu of music, links, news and community information would make most conventionally produced drama stick out like a sore thumb.

However, religious broadcasting does provide certain scope for using drama as long as it's professionally done and with a wide appeal. There's usually more speech content in religious programming, with the chance to develop issues and themes in a little more depth. Short sketches, voicers and conversation pieces can spotlight a topic or spice up a Pause for Thought in a unique way.

If you're involved in a local drama group whose members are talented, committed and flexible in their approach, and you'd like to offer your work to local religious broadcasters, do so by all means, but be prepared to ask yourselves the following questions:

1. Are you really as professional as you would like to think? What lots of church drama groups get away with in family services simply wouldn't be acceptable on radio.

2.   Radio stations are out to get as many listeners as possible—and in the case of ILR stations, to keep advertisers happy. Does the drama you offer entertain Christians and no one else?

3.   Have you taken the trouble to get to know those responsible for religious broadcasting in your local station? Many work under enormous pressures, with little or no money behind them, trying to meet the demands of programme controllers and churches both at the same time. It can be hard work, so find out how you can really be of service to them.

4.   Are you prepared to fit in with and use co-operatively the time and resources that may be offered to you? In most radio stations, it's a constant battle to get enough studio time, engineering help, tape, coffee—you name it. So patient contributors, with a sense of fun and who aren't looking for stardom, are a must.

5.   Are your scripts and production ideas really meant for *radio*? You can't bring on a useful visual at a dull moment, remember! Accents, characterisation through voice, and sound effects are vital. Most stations will have a good collection of sound effects records. Be willing to take technical and production advice on how to use them to best effect.

6.   Are you offering something new? Nothing excites a broadcaster more than an imaginative and fresh approach to something rather than ancient techniques and old jokes! If you can offer radio drama which is so communicative, compelling and entertaining that it just leaps out of the speakers at you, you'll be a welcome resource for local broadcasting.

If you are invited to do some radio work, it's as well to settle any queries about copyright, fees and payment in advance, and talk to the radio station about ownership of the material after broadcast. Legally the recording is theirs.

Val Ogden, Local Radio,
Religious Programmes Presenter

14. Rabbit, Rabbit

Putting the Boot In
by Alan MacDonald

Footprints Theatre Company has written and recorded several series for radio. The key to writing drama for this medium is to view radio's limitation as a potential advantage. If sound is the only dimension to our drama, then it can be set anywhere we wish, with any combination of characters and events, on any timescale we ordain.

The only rules are that the listener can clearly understand what is happening and that it stimulates his imagination to work. Feeding the imagination of your audience is what brings the extra dimension to radio drama. It could be called making pictures out of sound.

Consider the following radio sketch, addressing the subject of suffering, and see how its unusual situation demands the listener's imagination.

Characters: SKINHEAD, VICTIM

[SFX: *a football crowd. The noise of singing and chanting should continue throughout the piece. Over the top of this is heard a small group of supporters chanting ''ere we go'. They start far off and grow louder.*]
SKINHEAD: There's one, get him!
                [SFX: *sound of running, a scuffle and some-body out of breath.*]

	Got you, sunshine! You a City supporter?
VICTIM:	No. Argh!
SKINHEAD:	I said, you a City supporter?
VICTIM:	No!
SKINHEAD:	Then why you wearing this scarf then?
VICTIM:	What scarf? Eurgh! How did that get there?
SKINHEAD:	You've had it, sunshine, I'm going to do you good and proper.
VICTIM:	Are you?
SKINHEAD:	Definitely.
VICTIM:	That seems a bit of a waste of energy.
SKINHEAD:	You what?
VICTIM:	[*talking fast*] I mean, what good will it do, how will it benefit the human race?
SKINHEAD:	I'll enjoy it.
VICTIM:	Oh yeah, I dare say you'll enjoy it, but what will you have achieved? I mean, when I'm left here with my nose broken, several teeth missing and a number of cracked ribs, will you feel that my suffering has in some way contributed to the good of society?
SKINHEAD:	There'll always be suffering, won't there? Now shut up, you're spoiling my fun.
VICTIM:	Yeah, yeah, but ask yourself why? Why is there always suffering? I mean, I take it we're assuming the existence of a loving God?
SKINHEAD:	'Course. Do you take me for an atheist or something?
VICTIM:	Not at all, but think about it for a moment. If God is really omnipotent and he's created this world, why does he allow the amount of suffering that takes place? Why doesn't he put a stop to it?
SKINHEAD:	Perhaps he can't.
VICTIM:	Then he's not God.
SKINHEAD:	Perhaps he don't want to.
VICTIM:	Then he's not loving.

SKINHEAD: Oh, I dunno. Can't I just do you over and think about it later?

VICTIM: All right, go ahead, but you'll be committing an action without a sound theological basis.

SKINHEAD: Is that bad?

VICTIM: Bad as losing to Chelsea.

SKINHEAD: Stone me. Er... [*He is thinking.*] I've got it. Look at all the great art that's come out of suffering. I mean, Bunyan, Van Gogh, Mozart, McLeish.

VICTIM: McLeish?

SKINHEAD: Left back for United. Broke his leg last season.

VICTIM: Oh, come on, now. You can't justify the place of suffering in the world just because a few good books and pictures have come out of it, can you?

SKINHEAD: Can't you?

VICTIM: No! What about earthquakes, volcanoes, cancer, handicapped children?

SKINHEAD: Well, I dunno, do I? I'm not God. Now let's get on with it.

VICTIM: Ah, but what if you were? What if you were a loving God and you were standing here now? Would you be kicking an innocent person's head in?

SKINHEAD: Well, 'course not. Not if I was loving. I'd be more likely to lie down and let you have a go at me.

VICTIM: You're right! Go on then.

SKINHEAD: Oh. Hang on a bit then. [*He lies down.*] Is this all right?

VICTIM: Fine.

SKINHEAD: Ow! Argh! Oooh!
[*SFX: sound of someone being beaten up. Fades out.*]

15. Christmas Turkey

Three Brave Shepherds
by Alan MacDonald

This piece would be great fun at Christmas-time, perhaps as part of a carol service. The three shepherds can be male or female, but they must be played as larger-than-life country bumpkins. The whole piece lends itself to ham (or mutton) acting. A microphone offstage may be helpful for the voice of the angel.

Characters: ONE, TWO and THREE—all shepherds.
                         VOICE OF ANGEL

[*Enter shepherds, singing. They wear smocks and necker-chiefs and carry crooks.*]

ALL:	While shepherds watch their flock by night All seated on the ground... [*They pause, look at each other.*] La, la, la, la, la, la, la, la, La, la, la, la, la, la—
ONE:	We must think of an ending to that some-time.
TWO:	Well I don't think we're going to find 'er up 'ere.
THREE:	She's gone. Gone into that meadow up yonder.
TWO:	Up yonder where?

THREE:	Up yonder in the sky, you clod-face. I was speaking metabolicly.
TWO:	Oh.
ONE:	That's the third lamb we've lost this week.
TWO:	Ewe.
ONE:	Don't blame it all on me.
TWO:	No it was a ewe we lost.
ONE:	[*slow-witted*] A—ewe—we—lost. Ahaa, I've got you.
THREE:	Where?
ONE:	No, not a ewe, him. Forget it, let's get back to the hut.
TWO:	Right.
ALL:	This way. [*They set off in three different directions.*] I'm sure it was... But didn't we?...
THREE:	[*triumphantly*] I knew it! [*They look at him hopefully.*] We're lost!
ONE:	And there's a mist coming down. [*Eerily*] There's something I don't much like about this place. [*A pause. They look about them warily.*]
TWO:	[*loudly*] It reminds me...[*The other two jump.*] of when I was a lad tending my father's flock in the mountains. It was dark and there was a cold mist like this one. I was alone apart from the staff I always carried with me. When all of a sudden out of the mist came the howl of a wolf. Owww! I wheeled round, just in time to see it leap for my throat...and I felled it with one blow from my staff.
ONE:	A brave act, shepherd.
THREE:	[*after a pause*] A similar thing happened to me, just before my thirtieth birthday. I was searching for an old ram, the way we

are now, and I somehow got separated from my companions. The fog came down, and I took refuge in a cave. It was so dark in this cave you couldn't see your hand in front of your face, but I stumbled further inside to be out of the wind... when all of a sudden from the back of a cave I heard the growl of a she-lion. [*Feebly*] Grrrr! It came for me, snarling and spitting, knocked me to the ground, clawed my face till I bled as we wrestled together. I strangled it with my bare hands.

ONE: A brave act, shepherd. Not unlike the encounter I had only last winter. I had just got the last sheep into the fold and was counting up when I noticed my dog Ben was acting strange. He was a brave dog usually, but here he was cowering and whimpering like a puppy. I walked over to the trees where he'd come from and called him, [*shouts*] 'Ben!' 'cos that was his name, but he wouldn't come for any persuasion. Then there was a rustling in the trees, just briefly like. I stopped and listened... [*Long pause*] Nothing. [*Dramatically*] Then all of a sudden from out of the forest came...

[*Suddenly there is a great fanfare of noise— drums, cymbals, trumpets—whatever you can. This is heard from offstage. The brave shepherds cower together in a trembling heap while a heavenly voice is heard from offstage. They look upwards as if it is coming from the sky.*]

VOICE OF ANGEL: Why do you look so scared? I am here with good news for you. This very day in David's town your Saviour was born— Christ the Lord! And this is what will prove it to you: you will find the baby, wrapped in cloth and lying in a manger.

[*The three shepherds come out of their terrified huddle and look at each other dumbfounded.*]

THREE: I've got it! [*Sings*]
While shepherds watched their flocks by night
All seated on the ground
The angel of the Lord came down
And glory shone around.

ONE, TWO: No. It'll never catch on.
[*They all exit, arguing.*]

DESSERTS

16. Easter Eggs

Tipped to Win
by Steve Stickley

Amid the commercialisation of Easter according to the Gospel of Rowntree, Macintosh and Cadbury, this egg will leave a more lasting taste. It provides a very different approach to Christ's death. The fast moving, almost breathless pace provides its audience with a compelling image of the effect of materialism on our lives, and the way in which Christ literally stands up against the 'ways of all flesh'. **Tipped to Win** *will prove valuable in a variety of situations: church services, assemblies…even worth a try on the street (the addition of TV 'cameras' would certainly help draw a crowd). It is an excellent idea to study the commentary of the likes of Peter O'Sullivan to capture the flavour of this instantly recognisable genre. Be warned, though, a photographic memory for lines is an ideal prerequisite—it is very demanding in rehearsals, so give yourselves plenty of preparation time!*

Like Easter eggs, **Tipped to Win** *would also be welcomed at any time of the year.*

Characters: Both have a rather cynical attitude off-camera and an annoyingly vivacious one on-camera. TWO is more innocent than ONE who regards himself as an old hand at broadcasting. ONE is a man, TWO is a woman.

[*Both are seated, approximately two metres apart.* ONE *is smoking nervously,* TWO *is tidying her hair.*]

ONE: Actually they should be renewing my contract soon...

TWO: Good for you.

ONE: For the second time.

TWO: I've put in for promotion actually...

ONE: Good for you.

TWO: I'm sure to be short-listed.

ONE: I stand a good chance.

TWO: So do I.

BOTH: Good for you. [*Laugh. They both stand.* ONE *stubs out cigarette,* TWO *adjusts clothing. They take up their 'on-air' pose to their respective cameras and smile. Pause.*]

TWO: They're cueing us in.

ONE: Good afternoon from Leslie Bickering BBC Grandstand.

TWO: Hello there from Lesley Wittering ITV World of Sport.

BOTH: Welcome to Pay-docked Park for this afternoon's Rat Race.

ONE: The going is smooth...

TWO: The going looks good...

BOTH: For the 1989 Materalistic Cup

ONE: The turf is firm...

TWO: The weather is fine...

BOTH: For this afternoon's all-important fixture in the Rat Race season. [*They stand side by side DSC and look through mimed binoculars.*]

ONE: As they come to the start there's the favourite 'Grab-It-All' at 2 to 1, a thoroughbred out of 'Ready-Cash' and 'I'll-Pay-You-Back'.

TWO: Here comes 'Push-and-Shove' at 7 to 1, always a determined runner.

ONE:	It looks like being a good Rat Race today.
BOTH:	They're under starter's orders...and...they're off!

[*For the whole of the race section the actors should be contained within a small 'boxed' area with limited movements. They bob up and down with the action of the race.*]

TWO:	A good start from 'Grab-It-All' in the centre...
ONE:	On the far side 'It's-All-Mine' is looking strong...
TWO:	This could be a fast race.
ONE:	The pace is picking up as 'Get-Your-Hands-Off-Mate' makes a strong bid on the outside of the field.
TWO:	In the centre its 'I-Wanna-Be-Filthy-Rich'.
ONE:	'So-Do-I'.
TWO:	'So-Do-I' and 'Don't-We-All' bunching together on the rails.
ONE:	But at the front...
TWO:	It's 'Grab-It-All' from 'Push-And-Shove'...
ONE:	'It's-All-Mine' moving up to 'Grab-It-All'... he's always grabbing at something!
TWO:	'Get-Your-Hands-Off-Mate' is lying third— but then he's always lying!
ONE:	And there's a faller!
TWO:	'Snatch-It-Quick' has fallen!
ONE:	'Snatch-It-Quick', an outsider, has fallen into certain bankruptcy!
TWO:	That's him written off for this season anyway.
ONE:	So it's the favourite 'Grab-It-All' from 'Push-And-Shove'...
TWO:	'It's-All-Mine' dropping slightly as they turn the bend into Barclay's Bank...
ONE:	'Get-Your-Hands-Off-Mate' moving up on the outside...
TWO:	'Push-And-Shove' making a challenge...

[*They begin to squabble physically.*]

ONE:	'Grab-It-All' being threatened...

TWO:	It's 'Get-Your-Hands-Off-Mate'
ONE:	From 'Push-And-Shove' [*He shoves her.*]
TWO:	'Get-Your-Hands-Off-Mate' [*She pushes him.*]
ONE:	'Push-And-Shove' [*He blocks her view.*]
TWO:	'Get-Your-Hands-Off-Mate' [*She pushes him out of her way.*]
ONE:	'It's-All-Mine' is dropping back...
TWO:	'It's-All-Mine' is out of it—probably to redundancy or unemployment.
ONE:	That's a shame, but it's 'Push-And-Shove' leading the field...
TWO:	And 'So-Do-I' has fallen!
ONE:	'So-Do-I' is out of it. A very seasoned runner...
TWO:	Probably be retired to an old people's home now...
ONE:	A great shame... but at the front of the field...
TWO:	[*seeing something else in the opposite direction*] Hold on!
ONE:	It's 'Push-And-Shove'...
TWO:	There's someone on the course.
ONE:	...from 'Get-Your-Hands-Off-Mate'...
TWO:	Perhaps there's something wrong...
ONE:	They turn now into Mean Streak with the finish in sight...
TWO:	The idiot, what's he doing? He's walking towards the field!
ONE:	And 'I-Wanna-Be-Filthy-Rich'...
TWO:	I can't believe my eyes, why don't the stewards do something? They're ignoring him!
ONE:	'Don't-We-All' [*Continues with semi-audible comments ad lib.*]
TWO:	This is terrible... They'll flatten him! Watch out!
ONE:	Now it's 'Grab-It-All' challenged by 'Push-And-Shove' with 'Don't-We-All' on the outside...
TWO:	Get out of the way! [*She has moved immediately DS of ONE.*]

ONE:	'I-Wanna-Be-Filthy-Rich' pressing hard, but it's 'Push-And-Shove' with 'Don't-We-All' neck and neck from 'Grab-It-All' then 'Get-Your-Hands-Off-Mate'. [*He is now leaning on* TWO.] And a tricky moment there as they all pass over an obstacle on the course [*He pushes her onto the floor.*] it's 'Don't-We-All' running superbly from 'Push-And-Shove' followed by 'Grab-It-All'. Only yards to go now, it's 'Don't-We-All' all the way—a whole length clear of 'Push-And-Shove', look at him go! And at the post it's 'Don't-We-All' first, 'Push-And-Shove' second, a photo for third between 'Grab-It-All' and 'Get-Your-Hands-Off-Mate', and past the post in final position the young aspiring 'I-Wanna-Be-Filthy-Rich'...
TWO:	[*Getting up.*] He was trying to stop them.
ONE:	[*To camera as at beginning.*] So the winner of the 1989 Materialistic Cup is 'Don't-We-All'.
TWO:	They just crushed him.
ONE:	And what a fine race that was...
TWO:	They trampled him to death.
ONE:	'Don't-We-All' showing superb form. This is Leslie Bickering at Pay-docked Park. [*He relaxes.*]
TWO:	Look, look. He's getting up!
ONE:	You what?
TWO:	Look, that bloke—he's all right! I was sure he was dead.
ONE:	What are you talking about?
TWO:	Over there...he's going back to the fallers.
ONE:	[*looking through binoculars again*] Hmmm, some people will do anything to get on telly.
TWO:	Come on, let's find out what's going on.
ONE:	Hey, hey—we're commentators, we don't get involved, remember?
TWO:	But it's a miracle he's still alive!
ONE:	You start talking like that you'll end up doing

	Songs of Praise. All those old nags wearing religious blinkers and carrying extra weight.
TWO:	Yes...
ONE:	[*becomes over-avuncular*] There are more important things, I mean, you've got your promotion to think of...
TWO:	Yes, maybe you're right...
ONE:	Come on, I'll buy you a drink. [*Goes to exit, looks back, patronising.*] You need to get on in life.
TWO:	I need to get on in life.
ONE:	Don't we all? [*She looks at him. He smiles. They freeze.*]

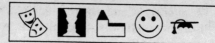

17. Trifle

Just Desserts
by Steve Stickley

Based closely on Matthew 24:45–51, this piece requires careful rehearsal of the mimed actions and vocal sounds. It proves particularly useful if you wish to involve the preacher or the person leading the service because of his or her interjection near the end. When it is finished the keys could be thrown to that person who may want to take the theme of 'things we have been entrusted with' or the Second Coming, using them as a tangible link. If this is not desired, the interjection should be provided by TWO.

Characters: ONE—executive type of trendy young
             woman, generous but firm.
             TWO—scruffy thicko.

ONE: I'm the boss of Just Desserts
           A wonderful eating place.
           There's ice-cream, apple pie and cake
           So come and stuff your face.
           [TWO *jumps up from audience.*]
TWO: 'Scuse me, please, I need a job.
           Just tell me what to do,
           I like it here at Just Desserts
           So can I work for you?

92

ONE:	[*to audience*] Can he be trusted? Will he do?
TWO:	[*to audience*] If only she could see I'm reliable through and through...
ONE:	You are? Then work for me!
TWO:	Great!—'ere! You was listening when I was talking to the audience—that's dramatic effect, that is...
ONE:	Sorry. Actually I could do with some time off work, this could be providential.
TWO:	Yer wot?
ONE:	Providential.
TWO:	Durr...is that anyfink to do wiv insurance?
ONE:	I can see you're a man to be trusted.
TWO:	You can?
ONE:	Yes, and what's more— I'll put you in charge of Just Desserts So here are the keys to the door. [*She throws a bunch of keys to* TWO.]
TWO:	Fanks, fanks, that's really...
ONE:	Neat? I thought you'd like the idea. Now, the food and wine must be served on time, Do you best 'til I get back here. [*She starts to exit.*]
TWO:	Oh Just Desserts, oh Just Desserts You are a dream come true! Cor, look at all this lovely grub...
ONE:	Remember what I told you to do. Right, I'm just off for a trifle...
TWO:	There's no need to go off for a trifle, there's one here. [*Pointing at imaginary food.*]
ONE:	Never mind. [*To audience*] I do hope he'll be OK, what do you think?
TWO:	Yer wot?
ONE:	Just talking to the audience...
BOTH:	Dramatic effect...
ONE:	[*to audience again*] I didn't say when I'd be

	back. I left him to get on with it. The question is, what did he get on with? As soon as my back was turned... [TWO *provides suitable mimed actions and vocal sound FX throughout the following*.]
TWO:	Glug, glug, glug, glug. Booze, booze hic! I can't lose, I'm the boss of this place And if customers won't pay double [*He 'breaks' bottle*.] I'll smash 'em in the face! Uh!
ONE:	[TWO *punctuates the end of each of the following lines with an action and noise*.] He melted the ice-cream, Scoffed all the cakes. Squashed the swiss rolls And laced the milk shakes. He beat up the staff, Thought it was funny. Locked all the doors And nicked all the money.
TWO:	[*stuffing his pockets*.] Great stuff!
ONE:	But he didn't expect me to come back just now. [*walks to* TWO.]
TWO:	I didn't expect you to come back just now. Aargh!
ONE:	Keys please. [TWO *nervously jangles the keys as he drops them into* ONE's *hand*.] Are you ready for your just deserts?
TWO:	But er... but er...
ONE:	Don't try to butter me up! [TWO *groans at the bad joke while* ONE *dons a suitable pair of glasses*.] The accused is hereby sentenced to thirty-five years hard labour in Her Majesty's Prison on the island of Noah's Cape. There he will set to work grinding up rocks... with his teeth.
TWO:	Not grinding my teeth! Please!

ONE:	[*taking off glasses*] That's what it says in the Bible. [*To audience*] In fact it is much worse, it actually says 'the boss cut him into little pieces.'
TWO:	Errr!
ONE:	If only he'd done what I asked, things would have turned out very differently. [*Struck by an idea*] Hey, let's run the film backwards!
TWO:	Huh? [*They both reverse every action and noise at top speed.*]
ONE:	Right, I'm just off for a trifle...
TWO:	There's no need to go off for a trifle, there's one here.
ONE:	Never mind. [*To audience*] I hope he'll be OK, what do you think?
TWO:	Yer wot?
ONE:	[*She hesitates then does double-take to* TWO.] Ever had that feeling of déjà vu? Anyway, I didn't say when I'd be back. I let him get on with it. As soon as my back was turned...
TWO:	Get out the food, get out the wine. Set all the tables, hope I've got time.
ONE:	[TWO *once again provides appropriate actions*.] He did the... Mixing-up, dishing-up, serving-up, washing-up, Adding-up, stacking-up,
TWO:	Crash!
ONE:	Broke a cup.
TWO:	Oh heck!
ONE:	Never mind. He did the... Peeling here, slicing there, chocolate sauce, banana, pear, Serving here, smiling there,
TWO:	Sit here, madam, crack!
ONE:	Broke a chair.
TWO:	Oh heck!

ONE: Never mind. But he didn't expect me to come back just now.

TWO: I didn't expect you to come...'til eight o'clock, madam, your table's right this way...

ONE: It's me!

TWO: It's you!

ONE: How did you do?

TWO: Very well thank you...actually... I broke a cup. I broke a chair... Never cleaned that cupboard under the stairs! But I hope it's all right.

ONE: All right? It's fine! The guests are all happy and the food is on time.

PREACHER: Excuse me!

TWO: [*a hint of panic in his eyes*] Yes, sir, your arctic roll is just on its way.

ONE: Well, nearly all the food is on time.

TWO: [*hands keys back as before*] I tried my hardest, worked my fingers to the bone... ooh they still hurts!

ONE: Keep the keys, I'm very pleased. This place is yours, your Just Desserts! [*She gives the keys to him.*]

TWO: [*overcome and embarrassed*] Aww! For me? [*More embarrassed gurgling*] Aww...well, I can't hang around here for dramatic effect...I've got an arctic roll to chase! [*He turns as if to exit and freezes.* ONE *shrugs to audience.*]

18. Ice Cream Sundae

Children's Workshop I

There can be little doubt about the value of participating drama for children. The biggest problem seems to be how to enable the adult leaders to play along as well! These ideas simply formalise, for your benefit, what children do naturally—play. Feel free to use them as they stand but, ideally, the aim is to provide you with methods from which you may devise other ideas using different subject matter.

Role play, as you will see, requires a lot of imagination on your part and although this example puts you into the role of a ship's captain or purser, it is important to bear in mind that you can often be 'yourself' and allow the children to develop your role alongside their own ideas. (See 'French Bread' p 128.)

Improvisation can take many forms. All it essentially means is play-acting. This example may be termed 'guided improvisation', ie developing a basic theme to give fresh insight into the passage at the end of the session. However, there is much scope for other approaches, eg starting with the passage and developing the children's ideas, or taking a character out of the Bible and putting him/her into a situation of the children's choosing.

When it comes to knowing the children you are the

'Allow the children to develop your role...'

expert, so use these suggestions as you wish. They may give new impetus for further experimentation.

Role Play: In the same boat

Aim: to provide a fresh insight into the story of Jesus stilling the storm.

You enter the room with a determined manner and a clip board. 'Good morning, ladies and gentlemen, welcome aboard the *QE2* for your Mediterranean cruise. I hope you have all managed to find your cabins and that your luggage has been delivered safely. Does anyone have a brown suitcase missing? One of our crew has found an unlabelled suitcase in the restaurant and I need to establish who it belongs to. Perhaps you could all check your luggage? I'm sorry to put you to this inconvenience but all unidentified objects must be investigated. Can I suggest you check your belongings before lunch in five minutes time? Thank you.'

What happens next depends on the children's reactions and your relationship with them. Maybe they are the type of group to take up the idea immediately— perhaps one or two of them will initiate action with others. If this is the case it would seem appropriate to remain in your role and encourage those who are a little slower to take up the idea. Maybe the children sit dumbstruck or embarrassed, in which case there's not going to be any action—perhaps it would be better for you to come out of role and ask them for their reactions. You should, however, aim to get them and yourself back in role as soon as possible. (It may be necessary to decide together on certain physical parameters, eg these chairs can be the restaurant, the lifeboats are over there by the window, etc.) Maybe the children need a little encouragement actually to get started—once they see your willingness to play along they'll play too.

That's the key to this approach. You must enter into the situation (or the 'play contract' you are offering) with 100 per cent conviction, and learn to accept and use the inevitable comments or thoughts of 'what's all this about?' that the children may actually express or show on their faces within the first few minutes. Whatever happens though, stay in role until *you* decide when to come out of it.

Use the children's ideas and let them initiate and build. Maybe the suitcase becomes a terrorist threat, or Becky decides it's the one she lost containing something very precious. Maybe the suitcase ceases to be important and another initiative develops, eg Christopher falls overboard.

For the benefit of this particular exercise you know in a few minutes that the hurricane will be introduced. The way in which you handle this is vital. Your aim is for the children to recreate the feelings of fear, and not to have them throwing themselves around, shouting their heads off and wrestling with sharks. So you may impose a discipline, eg 'Stay in your cabin with your family or friends—whatever happens, stay there. Decide what you are doing—playing cards, writing postcards—but stay there.' Then, perhaps as yourself, you quietly and slowly start to describe the weather changing, the boat listing a little, the frightened thoughts some may have. Inevitably a crescendo will build and you will have to decide when to stop—maybe the boat capsizes, maybe they all cram into a lifeboat.

Talk with your group about their reactions and thoughts about a storm at sea. Bring any historical or topical references into the discussion (eg the *Titanic*, *Herald of Free Enterprise*, etc.) Then ask if any of them can think of any boats and storms in the Bible. Read together Mark 4:35–41. Find out the size of the Lake of Galilee. Talk about the disciples' fears.

Try out this approach with other incidents or stories from the Bible, but always bear in mind that you must establish the three Cs:

1. Characters—who you and they are.

2. Context—where you and they are.
3. Concern—what the issue is.

After the initial section you must then determine how much 'rope' to give the children and whether other factors will be introduced later on. Finally, don't over-use role-play; once a quarter may be enough.

19. Ice Cream Sundae Split

Children's Workshop II
Improvisation: Holed Up

Aim: to involve junior-aged children in an imaginative exploration of the theme of injustice, and to provide a new insight into the story of Joseph and his brothers in Genesis 37.

1. Get the children into pairs to decide where they would like a hold-up to take place. After a few seconds ask around the group for their ideas. Explain that you would like one to be the criminal and the other to be the person in charge of the money or valuables. Emphasise that there is a bullet-proofed glass screen between them. The aim is for the one being robbed to dissuade the robber from committing their crime. After one or two minutes gather the children around and ask to hear some of their reasoning. The fact that the robber's intentions are unfair should emerge—if not, you ask: 'Why shouldn't a criminal steal money?' Explain that you are all going to look at the theme of 'it's not fair'.
(5–10 minutes)

2. Without warning or explanation hand out some Smarties (or similar sweet) to a random selection of children eg all those with dark hair or blue eyes, etc. Start to tell a real or imagined story from your own childhood about something unfair that happened to

you. Part way through hand out more Smarties to the same children, again without explanation. Continue your story as if you are genuinely intending to draw out a learning point from it. By now some of them may start commenting on the sweets, or lack of them. Ignore it, asserting your leader role by moving the children on to the next exercise.
(5 minutes)

3.　Assemble all the group in a large circle. Move around the outside touching the 'sweet' children on the shoulder. Tell all the others to sit down on the floor in the middle. When they are seated, give those standing another Smartie. Let any comments be freely made by the children, you simply ensure that both sets do as you instruct. Signal to those standing to follow you to the other end of the room where you huddle them together and whisper conspiratorially (you could secretly ask them why they think you are doing this). After a little while, hand out more Smarties to your secret group with the instruction to keep them in their hands behind their back. Move them all back to form a circle around the seated children again. Ask those in the middle to guess what you and your select group have decided to do to them. After appropriate comments signal to the other children to go round and share their sweets. As you ask the deprived ones how they felt and what they thought was going on, give them more Smarties.
(10–15 minutes)

4.　Ask the whole group to make comments about people they have heard of, or know, who are treated unfairly and why. Bring the discussion round to family relationships—especially brothers and sisters. Get them into threes to invent the most unfair thing some-one could do to their brother or sister. Briefly ask around to hear some of their ideas (filtering out the violent suggestions diplomatically) then tell them to act out what they have thought up. Visit each group during

the five minutes or so that you have given them to improvise and offer your ideas and help.
(15 minutes)

5. Arrange the children into groups of four. Get each group to set out a small circle of chairs. Explain that they are going to make up a story that follows this simple scenario:

> They are all brothers and sisters. One of them has something that the rest are very jealous of and they scheme to throw him/her down into the circle. They argue about whether to kill him/her but eventually decide on something else.

Emphasise the need to decide what this circle represents, eg a lift shaft in a deserted factory, a hole in the ground, a dungeon, etc, and also the cause of the jealousy. Encourage them to arrive at a definite ending. After about five minutes take it in turns to see each group's scene and comment positively on their efforts.
(15–20 minutes)

6. Make a large circle of chairs and get everyone to stand on one each. Describe a desert scene in a hot country, building the atmosphere. Ask for a few suggestions of things they might be able to see and hear. Describe next this large, deep hole in the ground that used to store water and how it was impossible for one person to get out if they fell, or was pushed, into it. Ask them

a) what it would feel like to be left there
b) if there is anyone they would ever want to throw in there and why.

After a brief discussion get everyone (you included) to climb into the hole and sit very still to listen to the desert sounds. Simply tell them the story of when Joseph found himself down a hole in the desert. Lead this into a prayer about rejection and isolation, finishing with the rescue—perhaps you could pull them out one by one!
(10–15 minutes)

Look back over these suggested activities and decide which elements have been used to help build up towards the final story. This has been achieved by taking the passage in Genesis 37 and working backwards asking such questions as 'What do I want the children to be thinking and experiencing at each stage?' At some point you must decide how much 'power' to give the children—if their improvisation is meaningful to them they will be caught up in imaginative play. How far will you let this go? The ideas, for example, from number 5 could result in a gruesome scene in a dungeon or gangs of crooks in warehouses. This should not be seen as a hindrance but used as an advantage; you must be ready to eke out the salient points about rejection, etc, whilst accepting and affirming their ideas.

Although the scenario in that same section gives only the bare bones of the Joseph incident, don't expect their stories to bear any resemblance. Their freedom to devise is important, as they will appreciate section 6 even more as they realise the intention behind the whole exercise.

20. Jungle Jelly

Samuli and Kerassa the Tiger
by Steve Stickley

*This story is designed to be used with a group of children
who participate in the chorus. Actions should be devised by
the storyteller for the children to do during the chorus, eg
long grass: waving forearms backwards and forwards; rope
bridge: slapping alternate thighs in time with the rhythm;
parrots: making talking bird shapes with both hands;
monkeys and the apes: scratching under one arm; big
stones: thumping chest three times. Your own variations
will no doubt give you more satisfaction! The children
should also repeat all the phrases about Samuli and Kerassa
after each chorus, eg (You) 'Now Samuli he was small,'
(Children) 'He was very very small,' and so on.*

*As with all good storytelling variety of pitch, pace and
volume is essential. It will help to learn the piece by heart
thereby enabling the storyteller to maintain eye contact
with the children. If you have a poor sense of rhythm this is
not for you. A suitable introduction for the children to learn
their responses will be needed.*

NARRATOR: Samuli and his father always walked the
jungle path
To fetch food from the village for his sisters
and his mother.

'Beware of Kerassa' his father always told
   him,
'Kerassa is a tiger with eyes of fire and
   teeth like daggers to satisfy
   his hunger.'
And they walked through the long grass
Swish swish swish
To fetch food from the village for his sisters
   and his mother.
Now Samuli he was small,
He was very very small.
And Kerassa he was big,
He was very very big.

Samuli and his father were returning from
   the village
When they saw Kerassa's eyes through the
   leaves of the jungle.
'Don't be afraid' his father said 'Just walk
   slowly by and do not look into his eyes.'
'Let's run!' Samuli whispered 'Quick,
   quick, let's run!'
'No,' said his father, 'Walk and Kerassa
   will not chase you.'
So they walked through the long grass,
Swish swish swish
Across the rope bridge [*Slap thighs three
   times.*]
Fetching food from the village for his
   sisters and his mother.
Now Samuli he was scared,
He was very very scared.
And Kerassa he was fierce
He was very very fierce.

Samuli asked his father why Kerassa was
   so fearsome
And his father started telling him the
   mysteries of the jungle;
How the God of all creation breathed upon

the soil
And made tigers to be hungry and boys to
be brave.
How the God of all creation made both the
strong and the weak,
The running and the walking in the green
green jungle.
'Kerassa he was fashioned to chase the
timid deer
And a little boy running looks just the
same,
So you must walk through the long grass
Swish swish swish
Across the rope bridge [*Slap thighs three
times.*]
Past the parrots in the trees
Squawk squawk squawk
and the monkeys and the apes
Chatter chatter chatter
To fetch food from the village for your
sisters and your mother.'
Now Samuli he was weak,
He was very, very weak,
And Kerassa he was strong,
He was very very strong.

Samuli had a dream as he was sleeping on
his mat
That he was walking through the jungle all
alone—on his own.
He didn't have his father and his strong
hand to hold,
When he heard a low growl from the dark
dark jungle.
'Grrr I am Kerassa with eyes of fire, teeth
like daggers to satisfy my hunger, Grrr.'
Samuli started running with his heart
beating faster
Hot tiger-breath on the back of his neck.

He ran through the long grass,
Swish swish swish
Across the rope bridge [*Slap thighs three
times.*]
Past the parrots in the trees,
Squawk squawk squawk
And the monkeys and the apes,
Chatter chatter chatter
Bringing food from the village for his
sisters and his mother.
Now Samuli was frightened,
He was very very frightened.
And Kerassa he was near,
He was very very near.
But it was only a dream.

Samuli woke up quickly and early in the
morning
And went to wake his father to fetch food
for the day.
But his father lay there moaning and
crying in a fever;
'Samuli, go alone' his mother gently told
him,
'Learn to be brave as you walk through the
jungle,
For the God of all creation knows Kerassa
and this fever
And the little boy who learns to be bold.'
So he walked through the long grass
Swish swish swish
Across the rope bridge [*Slap thighs three
times.*]
Past the parrots in the trees
Squawk squawk squawk
And the monkeys and the apes
Chatter chatter chatter
Stepping on the big stones [*Thump chest
three times.*]

To fetch food from the village for his
    sisters and his mother.
Now Samuli he was brave.
He was very very brave.
And Kerassa he was hungry,
He was very very hungry.

Samuli was returning on the path through
    the jungle
When darkness came upon him like a
    cloak of fear.
Eyes of fire seemed to burn upon Samuli
And the silence of the jungle called the
    little boy to stop.
Crackling and rustling through the tangle
    of the jungle
Teeth-daggers gleaming and eyes all
    aflame crept Kerassa.
Samuli thought 'Run! Run for your life!'
But the God of all creation whispered
    'Listen to your father
And walk through the long grass
Swish swish swish
Across the rope bridge [*Slap thighs three
    times.*]
Past the parrots in the trees
Squawk squawk squawk
And the monkeys and the apes
Chatter chatter chatter
Stepping on the big stones [*Thump chest
    three times.*]
Bringing food from the village for your
    sisters and your mother.'
Now Samuli he was safe,
He was very very safe.
And Kerassa was still hungry,
He was very very hungry.

Next day Samuli went with his father
    through the jungle

And there on the path were the footprints
  he had made.
But there right beside them all along the
  pathway
Kerassa's paws had trodden following
  Samuli.
'I kept on walking,' Samuli told his father,
'I didn't try to run and I didn't look back.'

And now the years have come and gone,
  Samuli is a father
Taking his son along the dark jungle path.
They always walk through the long grass
  [*Whisper.*]
Swish swish swish
Across the rope bridge [*Slap thighs three
  times.*]
Past the parrots in the trees
Squawk squawk squawk
And the monkeys and the apes
Chatter chatter chatter
Stepping on the big stones [*Thump chest
  three times.*]
To fetch food from the village for his
  sisters and his mother.
Now Samuli he is wise
He is very very wise.
And Kerassa he is dead,
He is very very dead. [*Pause*]

But Kerassa leaves a son with eyes of fire
  and teeth like daggers
Kacheera is his name and he's the tiger of
  the jungle.
So you must never [*Increasing speed of
  chorus.*]
Run through the long grass
Swish swish swish
Across the rope bridge [*Slap thighs three
  times.*]

111

Past the parrots in the trees
Squawk squawk squawk
And the monkeys and the apes
Chatter chatter chatter
Stepping on the big stones [*Thump chest
    three times.*]
Fetching food from the village for your
    sisters and your mother.

21. Rhubarb, Rhubarb

Listen for a Change
by Steve Stickley

Listen for a Change was originally written for a large group of children to perform in a family service on the theme of responding to the cry of the poor. Almost any number may be employed as the chorus, and a simple skipping-type rhythm involving hand movements or finger clicking, etc, could prove very effective. Pointing to ears and mouth is essential to the success of the rhyming sections.

Characters: CHORUS—as many children as you can fit into the available space! Out of these, numbers ONE, TWO, THREE, FOUR provide the other voices.

CHARLIE—a worried young lad.

LUCY—a self-assured entrepreneur, aged eleven or so.

BEVERLEY—a selfish schoolgirl.

TINA—a worried schoolgirl.

Also in CHORUS when not performing

[*The* CHORUS *stand USC. A desk with a sign 'Psychiatric help, 5p,' is MSL with one chair behind for* LUCY *and another chair SR of desk for* CHARLIE. *A small table with a telephone is MSR.*]

CHORUS: One mouth, two ears,
                 Do you talk or do you hear?
                 One mouth, two ears,
                 Which do you do the most of?
                 We all need some persuasion
                 Listen please to our equation:
                 This is one and these are two [*They indicate mouth then ears.*]
                 And here's some sound advice for you,

ONE: The number of these to this is double
                 Too much of this is double trouble!

CHORUS: One mouth, two ears,
                 Do you talk or do you hear?
                 One mouth, two ears,
                 Which do you do the most of?
                 [*During the last chorus* LUCY *has moved to her desk. She sits polishing her nails and chewing gum.* CHARLIE *enters, worried.*]

CHARLIE: Can you help me?

LUCY: Well, that depends on you. Can you help yourself? Are you willing to help yourself? Do you know what self-help means? When you say 'help' is it a cry from the heart or simply a way of starting a conversation? Five pence please.

CHARLIE: Hang on! You haven't done anything yet. I wanted to know if you could help me with my problem?

LUCY: Ah, yes, a problem, a difficulty, a hurdle, an annoying obstacle...

CHARLIE: Yes! It's me mum, she's always shouting at me.

LUCY: [*sitting back, sympathetic*] Tell me about it.

CHARLIE: Ah, that's more like it. Well, you see, I find

114

	my mum very difficult to live with...
LUCY:	Who doesn't? Mine's a real pain, always putting my clothes into drawers when I wanted them on the floor. She's forever telling me to do things when I'm busy watching the video. She doesn't know when to stop...
CHARLIE:	Wait a minute, we're supposed to be talking about *my* mum.
LUCY:	Carry on...I'm here to help.
CHARLIE:	Right...well, when she shouts at me I shout back...
LUCY:	So do I! I tell her I'm grown-up enough to make my own decisions. In fact I often take the trouble to point out where she's gone wrong in life—but she doesn't appreciate it...[CHARLIE *is becoming agitated.*]...She's always telling me to shut up. Well I mean, that's no way to treat a sensitive child like me...
CHARLIE:	SHADDUP!
LUCY:	That's it, get angry. I always do, it's the only way to make her listen. Huh! Mothers...who needs them? They should be seen and not heard...
CHARLIE:	WILL YOU LISTEN TO ME?
LUCY:	That's just what my mum says to me! No self-control. Disgraceful behaviour for an adult. [CHARLIE *is seething through clenched teeth.*] That'll be five pence please. [CHARLIE *leaps up and attempts to throttle her.*]
CHARLIE:	AARGH!! [*Brief pause. They return during the next chorus.*]
CHORUS:	One mouth, two ears, Do you talk or do you hear? One mouth, two ears, Which do you do the most of?
TWO:	Before this trapdoor starts to squeak,

THINK!
Am I quick to listen and slow to speak?

CHORUS: One mouth, two ears,
Do you talk or do you hear?
One mouth, two ears,
Which do you do the most of?

[*During the last chorus* TINA *enters and picks up the telephone.* BEVERLEY *has moved to CS and is trying to write in a notebook.*]

CHORUS: Dring dring!
BEVERLEY: Oh, not now, I'm busy.
CHORUS: Dring dring!
BEVERLEY: I'm in the middle of my homework.
CHORUS: Dring dring!
TINA: I hope Beverley's in.
CHORUS: Dring dring!
TINA: Beverley's clever, she'll help me.
CHORUS: Dring dring!
BEVERLEY: I bet that's Tina.
CHORUS: Dring dring!
BEVERLEY: Wants me to help her as usual.
CHORUS: Dring dring!
BEVERLEY: She's a pain.
CHORUS: Dring dring!
TINA: Come on Beverley...
CHORUS: Dring dring!
TINA: Please answer...
CHORUS: Dring dring!
TINA: Please help me...
CHORUS: Dring dring!
BEVERLEY: Go away, Tina!
CHORUS: Dring dring!
TINA: Maybe she's out... [*She puts the telephone down and sadly walks back to* CHORUS.]
BEVERLEY: Good. That's better. Now then, nearly finished. [*She reads.*] 'If it takes twenty-four men three weeks to eat twelve tons of spaghetti with a teaspoon, how long would

it take three women to eat *thirty-four* tons of spaghetti with a knitting needle?' Bloomin' 'eck, that's impossible...I know, I'll ask Luigi. He knows all about spaghetti. [*She goes to the telephone.*] Four, eight, seven nine, two. He's bound to know.

CHORUS: Dring dring!
BEVERLEY: Luigi's clever, he'll help me.
CHORUS: Dring dring!
BEVERLEY: I hope he's in...
CHORUS: Dring dring!
BEVERLEY: This maths homework is awful!
CHORUS: Dring dring!
BEVERLEY: Please answer...
CHORUS: Dring dring!
BEVERLEY: Please help me...
CHORUS: Dring dring!
BEVERLEY: Please!
CHORUS: Dring dring!
            Dring dring!
BEVERLEY: I hope your spaghetti gets knotted! [*She slams the phone down and freezes.*]
THREE: If you refuse to listen to the cry of the poor...
FOUR: Your own cry for help will not be heard.
THREE: Proverbs twenty-one.
FOUR: Verse thirteen. [BEVERLEY *returns to* CHORUS.]
CHORUS: One mouth, two ears,
            Do you talk or do you hear?
            One mouth, two ears,
            Which do you do the most of?
THREE: If you've got a brain, then think.
ONE: If you've got a pair of feet, then walk.
TWO: If you've got a pair of hands, then help.
THREE: And if you've got a pair of these...[*All indicate ears. Slight pause.*]
ALL: DON'T TALK!

117

22. Angel Whispers

Window on the World
by Steve Stickley

*This short piece is crammed full of olde Englishe goodness.
Best used as a part of church worship for adults, its lyrical
style and use of music should blend in happily with the most
traditional service. The two actors perform in front of a
large white flat upon which is directed coloured light to give
the impression of a stained-glass window. This is best
achieved by back projection, the flat being an open frame
covered by white fabric. Both actors are dressed in black as
though silhouetted. Taped music is used and must be
sufficiently amplified for the final voice-over to be clearly
audible.*

*Thomas Tallis's 'Spem in Alium' is the ideal choice, and
the piece has been written to fit into the first four minutes
before the first climax of the movement. The voice-over
may then be provided live with a microphone from offstage
or, better still, dubbed onto the music at a louder level.
Careful work by a director on the varied use of voice will
greatly benefit the performance.*

*A suitable introduction may be needed such as: 'If those
people we see in stained-glass windows could speak, I
wonder what they'd have to tell us?'*

Characters: ONE—female
              TWO—male

Both wear contemporary but unobtrusive black clothing.

[*Music begins in blackout. Lights come on the screen to
reveal the actors silhouetted in profile.* ONE *is standing,*
TWO *kneeling, both in adoration, hands slightly raised.
They imagine the ascended Christ between them above
their heads. Movement throughout is minimal, slow and
deliberate. Front of house lights, if available, fade up
approximately eight seconds into the music.*]

ONE: Full thousand years have we stood
         Adoring Christ within this glass.

TWO: And thus our coloured window gives
         The light of life to those who pass
         In and out of this cathedral
         Staring upward to the light.

ONE: Full thousand year 'twixt earth and heav'n
         Have we proclaimed the risen Christ.
         [*Both turn their heads slowly DS as though
         looking into the cathedral.*]
         Worshippers kneel, whisper, breathe
         The sanctum of stone solemnity,

TWO: And then we see them rise and leave
         To a world weary of enmity.
         And still they come returning in
         To seek the peace of sanctuary

ONE: Girls turned women, boys to men,
         Full thousand year of prayer matured
         From cradle soft to friendless grave.

TWO: The men, the women, the children yearn
         Their feeble efforts for eternal praise,

ONE: And every face and heart that opes
         Its innermost and utter hope
         Finds the Christ who draws their love
         Into a Body glorified. [*She looks up at Christ
         again.*]

119

TWO: Such mystery of transformation
           Takes the fear of lostness caught
           Within the snarl of animal confusion,

ONE: To the dignity of fragile spirit raised [TWO
           looks up at Christ.]
           Within the wholesome palms of Christ
           Where its hope is born anew.
           [*During the next section they turn heads, then
           bodies, slowly DS relaxing arms slightly.*]

TWO: We see not preoccupation of whim or fancy
           Nor foolhardiness of human toil,

ONE: We see not mere men and women
           Nor children incapable of reverent praise.

TWO: We see not frustration, sadness, loss,
           Nor ineffectual good desire. [*He sits slowly
           back on his heels.*]

ONE: We see not the tiredness, doubt, confusion
           Nor weary minds and hearts grown faint.

TWO: We see not the agèd body weak of effort

ONE: Nor drainèd spirit deprived of hope.

TWO: For here we view a thousand years of myriad
           voices
           Crying out in praise and power, [*They both
           slowly return to their original positions.*]

BOTH: A million, million songs of love

ONE: Who gaze upon our Saviour! [*Pause*]

TWO: While sunshine spears through Jesu's side

ONE: To fall full hope upon each face

TWO: Mere human lives transformed and made

ONE: Into soldiers of mighty grace! [*They turn
           heads only DS.*]

TWO: We see rank on rank of armèd warrior
           Carry the sword into the world.

ONE: Through their weakness; through their pain
           They conquer like an army taken

BOTH: On from glory unto glory
           In the shadow of the Christ!
           [*They face upwards, still DS. The climax starts*

	to build.]
ONE:	And thus we see God's arm laid bare
TWO:	To work his will upon this earth.
ONE:	Each tiny life is given strength
BOTH:	To make the glorious kingdom come! [*They turn heads back to Christ. There is a slight pause as the musical climax swells then quietens.*]
VOICE FX:	Your strength is my love.
	Go, and proclaim it,
	Armed with this truth.
	[*Lights then music fade out.*]

23. Home made cakes

Writing

Take one pinch of inspiration, several cups of coffee, a packet of biros, six pages of foolscap (some shredded), mix together with a liberal helping of prayer, grease with perspiration, and turn into a play. Leave to bake in the imagination overnight.

If only it were that simple. Unfortunately, this chapter cannot give you a foolproof recipe for becoming a writer. If finding the correct ingredients were the only thing necessary we could all be Shakespeare, but however much you may analyse the Bard's work, the fact will remain that he had a gift for writing that you may not possess.

So what is the point in offering a chapter on this subject if it is a gift you either have or you don't? The reasoning is that if you have the talent, it can always be improved, and if you don't, attempting some of the exercises suggested below will perhaps forewarn you and save some unsuspecting audience from a painful experience!

The ability to write good drama is probably a less common skill than is often supposed, and if you sincerely doubt that you can write, it may be more profitable for you to consider the ideas offered on improvisation as a creative process (see p 136). If undeterred, you still think you may be a writer, there are four activities which you can be pursuing:

1. *Reading.* Any craftsman is familiar with the tradition of his craft and there is no better way to learn than by reading the work of accomplished playwrights. If the names Pinter, Beckett, Ibsen, Stoppard, Aeschylus and Marlow sound to you like the team-sheet for a European cup tie, then it is likely you are not ready to put pen to paper just yet.

2. *Watching.* Plays are meant to be performed, and watching good, bad, or indifferent drama at the theatre can offer great insights into what actually works on stage.

3. *Writing.* As in any craft, the only way really to improve is by doing it and then by doing it again.

4. *Receiving criticism.* What every writer hates, but without which he is lost. To avoid developing paranoia, it is probably best to find one or two people whose judgement you respect and listen to their criticism of your work.

Exercises for Writers

Style 1

A good exercise is to take a simple nursery rhyme and rewrite it in other forms. You may try Humpty Dumpty as a sports report, a romantic or horror story, a letter of complaint, or a party political broadcast. The possibilities are endless.

Style 2

A man enters a bank and threatens the cashier with a gun. He then notices the cashier is his ex-girlfriend. While they are reminiscing about old times, the police arrive and arrest him. Use the simple plot of this sketch, and try writing it in the style of another playwright, eg Pinter, Shakespeare, a Greek Tragedy.

'It is important to be able to accept criticism'

Photos

From magazines cut out a selection of photos that offer intriguing images and then see if you can write a scene that depicts what has taken place up to the moment of the photograph. Don't attempt to make a point, but concentrate on arousing the curiosity of your audience.

Parables

Although these are in danger of being done to death by Christians, writing your own version of a parable is still a good exercise in effective communication. Ask yourself: What was Jesus trying to convey in this parable? What might be the equivalent of the images he used today? (The parable of the sower might become the parable of the paper-boy.) Try attempting some of the less popular parables such as the parable of the Fig Tree, or the Talents.

Starters

Below is a table giving suggested themes and possible styles for dramatising them. The idea is to attempt each theme in up to four different styles. For example, David and Goliath could be written in Japanese culture as a martial arts combat (with subtitles perhaps!), or as a boxing match with commentary, or as the fairytale of 'David and the Giant', or taking the unusual angle of allowing Goliath to narrate the story. Besides an Old Testament and New Testament story, I have deliberately suggested a theme with many interpretations, 'Love', and one which is not in the Bible, but which raises important issues about honesty and image.

Theme	In another culture	Sports event	Fairy tale	A narrator in character
David and Goliath				
Love				
Zaccheus				
Job inter- views				

NB   All these exercises are to help you sharpen your writing skills. Do not assume that everything you write has to be performed.

Is it any good?

With a piece of finished writing in front of you, this question will immediately flash across your mind. If it doesn't, I would suggest you are probably not the stuff writers are made of.

It is true that excellence in writing, as in art, is a matter of opinion, but if generalisations can help, there are some qualities which mark good drama out from bad. It may be useful to re-read something you have written to see if any of these are lacking:

1.   *Conflict* is at the heart of most theatre; it opposes ideas, people or countries and without it there is little that is dramatic.
eg
JESUS: Sell all your possessions
MAN: Oh, all right
2.   *Action* is as important as words. If you have not given as much thought to what is happening on stage as to what is being said, then your audience will quickly become bored.
3.   *Truth*. We of all people should pay most attention to this, but we are constantly putting words into our characters' mouths that they would not really say, eg
MAN: Then it's true that Jesus has died for my sins and if I call upon Him now he will forgive me, even though I am a sinner?
OTHER MAN: Yes.

Finally, most accomplished writers are not satisfied with what they've produced until the fourth or fifth draft. Let us offer God our very best!

SIDE DISH

24. Fresh baked bread

A Role-Play Bible Study

'I can't act, I'm too inhibited,' people often say. Yet in everyday life each one of us has many roles that we play according to the situation: mother, friend, son, teacher, employee, customer, confidante...the list is endless and we accept all these roles naturally. The nature of role-play is simply to undertake other roles that we might not normally find ourselves in.

Role-play must be immediately distinguished from acting a character. If you are asked to act the character of a traffic-warden, you worry about how to portray the voice, walk and mannerisms of a traffic warden. If you are playing the role of a traffic warden, you are simply yourself, placed in the imaginary situation of writing tickets for illegally-parked cars.

The American Indians said it was necessary 'to walk in someone else's moccasins' to understand them. This phrase perfectly encapsulates the value of role-play. Through it we are able to see from somebody else's point of view, to appreciate a situation from an entirely new angle, and perhaps to gain a fresh perspective in the process.

Christians, sadly, have been hitherto so preoccupied with the performance aspect of drama that they have neglected the infinite potential of drama in learning

and discovery. Outside the church, drama is being used increasingly in counselling, psychiatry and drama therapy. Inside the church, the 'can't act, too inhibited' majority are led to believe that drama has nothing to offer them.

The following is just one example of how role-play could be explored by a group with no previous acting experience. There are other possibilities which will be mentioned at the end of the section, but here we will concentrate on how role-play can open a door for us to enter into a passage of the Bible.

How often have you heard people complain the Bible seems dry and lifeless to them? Here is a method of bringing a biblical story into the present so that we can see, feel and participate in it. If we can recapture some of the immediacy of this narrative, and experience even a degree of the wonder, surprise or disbelief of the original witnesses, then surely we will start to read the Bible with fresh eyes.

Role-Play Exercise—The Man Born Blind

Any role-play needs careful direction, and these notes are written for the leader of the exercise. It can be used with a group of between seven and twelve participants, irrespective of age or ability.

First read the passage in John 9:1–12, which sets the story in context. Explain that the group are going to take on certain roles within the story to explore it. It will be necessary at the outset to reassure them that no acting ability is needed and to talk about the distinction between role-play and acting a character.

It's also important that the group bring honest, spontaneous response to their roles and are not hampered by prior knowledge of the biblical record. Emphasise that the role-play takes place in the present and they must forget any idea that they know what happens next.

Lastly, explain that there will be times you ask them to come out of their role and be themselves again as we will explore the story in gradual stages.

The leader will later take the role of the chief Pharisee, but is neutral to begin with. His first job is to give out cards assigning each person a role to play.

Role-play Cards

1.   The man born blind (1 card) (Choose an imaginative member of the group.) 'You have always been blind although now you are in your thirties. You spend most of your time begging outside the Temple. People despise you because they consider your blindness a result of your sin or your parents'.'

2.   The man's parents (2 cards) (Choose a man and a woman.) 'You are both in your fifties. You are ashamed of having a blind son because people say it is a result of your sin. You have other children who are healthy. You regularly attend the synagogue and fear and respect the Pharisees.'

3.   Pharisees (2–5 cards) 'You believe in the absolute authority of the Mosaic Law and spend your time studying and applying it. You particularly stress tithing and observance of the Sabbath and are opposed to any new teaching or teachers. It is your duty to ensure the ordinary Jews keep the Law.'

4.   Bystanders (1–3 cards) 'You live/work in Jerusalem. You can choose to be anything from a beggar to a judge. You have heard many rumours about the man Jesus and are curious to meet him.'

When each person has been given a card allow five minutes for them to think out the background of the role they are playing. Stress that they don't have to act a character, but adopt another person's point of view. They should ask themselves questions like: What is my name? Am I married? What do I do during the day? What is my favourite food? How do I feel about the Romans? etc (ie anything that gives them a clearer idea of their identity).

Now put everyone in pairs, mixing up the different roles as much as possible. Divide the pairs into A and B. For the next five minutes A stays in his role and B must ask him questions about himself such as the above. A must always give an answer that seems to fit with the role he is playing. B is not 'in role' when asking questions.

After five minutes swap over so A is now asking B questions for another five minutes. Stop and let everyone come out of role.

Next, blindfold the person playing the role of the blind man, and put him in the charge of his parents. For the following ten minutes they are to lead him around the house with the blindfold on. This should be done in silence so that communication between them relies on touch. At first the parents should allow the blind man to gain confidence by guiding him carefully, but eventually they should encourage him to attempt harder things such as going upstairs, crawling under obstacles, washing his hands, etc.

This may provoke some hilarity but the aim is to discover the difficulties of being blind and to build a relationship of trust between the blind man and his parents.

Meanwhile, put the others into two groups, of Pharisees and Bystanders. For the next exercise they are to stay in their roles for ten minutes and have a group discussion. They have heard that Jesus has healed a blind man in their locality and they must give their reactions to this rumour.

Each group must ultimately decide what they want to do about Jesus. (Stress that it is their decision, they don't have to adhere to events recorded in the Bible.) In their discussion, they should adopt the procedure of each person introducing themselves by their name and status before speaking.

When the ten minutes is up, bring the blind man and

his parents back and stop discussion. Everyone except the blind man can now come out of role. Ask him to keep his eyes closed and the rest of the group to stay quiet. It is important now to allow the blind man some sense of the miracle that occurred.

Say to the group, 'This is what happened to the blind man, although none of you saw it take place.' Take off the blindfold, moisten your fingers and touch his eyes saying, 'Open your eyes and see.' Allow a brief pause, without breaking the quiet, then ask him to wait outside because the Pharisees wish to question him about what has happened. Ask the parents also to go to another room to decide on their story if the Pharisees should wish to question them.

Ask the remaining group to arrange themselves, seated in a circle. Explain that they are now to have the chance of questioning the blind man and his parents. You will now take on the role of Chief Pharisee and will be in control of the interrogation. Everyone is to stay in role as soon as you enter the circle and remain so until you move outside it. Again each person should introduce himself before speaking.

Enter the circle, leading the man who was blind and announce, 'This is the man who claims to have had his sight restored by the Galilean, Jesus. It is our responsibility to decide what to do with him as citizens and Pharisees of Jerusalem. Who wishes to ask him the first question?' Let the questioning take its course with you as chairman. When you think you have allowed enough time for everyone to have their say, ask one of the other Pharisees to fetch the man's parents. The interrogation should then proceed, cross-questioning the man and his parents.

Finally, when the discussion is not advancing any further, ask the assembled group to decide what to do with this man. Sum up whatever decision is reached and then step out of the circle, saying that the role-play is at an end. Allow ten minutes to talk about the feelings, differences and difficulties that the role-play aroused. This is a vital part of the role-play process.

Read the account in John 9:13–38 of what took place in the original story. You may want to conclude with a mini Bible study, considering questions such as:

1. What stages did the blind man pass through on his way to worshipping Jesus? (v 38)
2. What motivated the Pharisees' unbelief?
3. Why were the parents unable to rejoice in the miracle?
4. If you had been a bystander at the time, how would you have responded?
5. Do you testify to Jesus changing you in public life?

Other possible role-play situations are:

1. Jesus' encounters with people, eg the woman of Samaria, Zacchaeus, the rich young ruler, etc.
2. Old Testament characters, eg Moses, Joseph, David. Consider key conflicts in their lives.
3. Social issues, eg abortion, AIDS, the nuclear question. You could for instance, set up a committee of social workers, clergy, friends and relatives to help a pregnant sixteen-year-old decide whether to have an abortion.

DRINKS

25. Cocktails

Improvisation

A practical drama session for drama groups who are already working together. An opportunity to develop your own home-grown ideas to throw into the general cooking pot.

Aim: to feed a group's creativity and provide an opportunity for improvisational work of intrinsic value.

Lah dee dah

Tell the group to kneel down in a circle on the floor with one shoe in front of each of them. During the following rhyme, which is chanted together, each person takes the shoe in their right hand and moves it to the right, ie in front of the next person in the circle, on each 'dah'.

Lah dee dah
Lah dee dah
Lah dee dah dee dah dee dah.

On the last line the shoe is not released until the final 'dah'. It is placed in front of the person on the right on the first 'dah', back to the position in front of self on the second 'dah', then released on the final 'dah' in front of the next person. (It's easier than it sounds!) The stress on each 'dah' can be emphasised by banging the shoes

on the floor. Practise in unison, aiming to increase the speed. (If you are coping with this very well, try doing it to the left using the left hand, and then alternating right then left, etc.) Be warned, it is addictive!
(10 minutes)

Fortunately/Unfortunately

Arrange the group into threes. One person makes any spontaneous statement, eg 'I got up early this morning.' The next person follows on immediately with a logical counter to the statement starting with 'unfortunately...' For example, 'Unfortunately it was half-past two.' The third person continues with a 'Fortunately' statement: 'Fortunately I needed to be up to feed my goldfish...' Each then continues alternating in this way, maintaining a logical sequence throughout. Push each trio to increase the speed. A good game for encouraging spontaneous thinking.
(5 minutes)

What if/Well then

Each couple stands about one metre apart. One person starts with another spontaneous thought this time beginning 'What if'. For example, 'What if I suddenly turned into an alien?' The other replies with a spontaneous 'well, then' answer: 'Well, then you could star in a sci-fi film.' The first carries on: 'What if I accidentally zap all the film crew stone dead?' 'Well, then...' And so on. Again speed is of the essence. Swap over after a couple of minutes.
(5 minutes)

Instant Stories

In order for this to work your group needs to be familiar with the storytelling game in 'Paté Cake' (page 28). Try the exercise without any numbering, emphasising the need for sensitivity to allow whoever wants to take over telling the story to do so. Encourage them to listen and

Lah Dee Dah

build on each other's contributions. Repeat it a couple more times giving them a literary genre for them to follow, eg, an Enid Blyton story, Mills and Boone, Edgar Allan Poe, etc. Then briefly compare the differing vocabularies and atmospheres.
(15 minutes)

Take-Away

Sit the group in a large circle. Explain that everyone will be attempting instant improvisations using the skills of quick thinking, co-operation, sensitivity, etc, required so far. Ask for two volunteers to go into the middle. The scene is set in any type of take-away. You explain that the two will begin as they wish. As they go on members of the group have the freedom to shout out words/ideas which the two in the middle must incorporate, eg, objects, emotions, environmental conditions, etc. Point out the need for those around the circle to watch as well as suggest ideas. Give everyone a turn in the take-away and encourage applause and praise. Set your own time limit to each improvisation—a minimum of two minutes. Discuss the work, underlining the need for co-operation.
(15–30 minutes)

Uncomfortable Conjunctions

Again group members will improvise in pairs (different partners) with the rest watching. Give everyone thirty seconds to think of a setting for themselves, eg fishing off a pier, having a shower, putting in bedding plants, etc. The pair must then improvise a scene together whilst both remaining true to their choice of setting. (They may select a second choice if a preceding improvisation has already used their original idea.) Again underline the need for co-operation and for each pair to find a 'middle ground' in what happens and try to bring it to a satisfying conclusion. No conferring is permitted beforehand. Discuss briefly after each one, highlighting pleasing moments or, perhaps, noting how the choice of phrasing became more ambiguous in order to incorporate each other's ideas. Also point out where any undermining may have taken place, eg 'Oi! What are you doing pretending to have a shower on the end of this pier?'

If the exercise has worked well the group will probably want to attempt more, changing partners again. There is also great value in repeating scenes in order to give the actors the opportunity to refine and/or explore further. Either way, you will find this great fun and very challenging. Take notes of good ideas that emerge. (20–40 minutes)

Discuss possibilities for further unusual conjunctions to feed the group's imagination, eg Moses in Boots the Chemist, Noah and the Ark on the roof of the *Tomorrow's World* studio, Goliath joins Ballet Rambert, etc. (5–10 minutes)

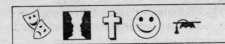

26. Pop!

One of the Crowd?
by Steve Stickley

Suitable for children to watch or even perform, this short piece may be used as part of a family service on a theme that looks at the importance of being ourselves as God created us, or the need to stand out against the way of the world. Essential equipment are two sets of brightly coloured, large, plastic 'popper-beads', the type suitable for young infants. Each bead is approximately nine centimetres long, hollow and squeezable, so as to create a vacuum when placed on the skin! Investigate your local toyshop, Early Learning Centre or the crèche. Actions should be devised with the beads to suit the script, with the accent on fun. The pace is fast moving and the rhythm should be maintained wherever possible.

Characters: ONE—male
              TWO—female

[ONE *and* TWO *enter clicking fingers to a regular beat. The popper beads are hung around their necks. During the following opening section the beads are used as indicated at the end of each line.*]

ONE: Do you like fast cars? [*Steering wheel*] Brrm brrm!
TWO: Do you like to take the train? [*Blowing into one bead*] Peep peep!

ONE: Do you watch loads of telly? [*Looking through a screen*] Duhh duhh!

TWO: Do you moan about the rain? [*Umbrella*] Grrr rrr!

BOTH: [*having slipped beads back round neck, clicking fingers*]
Don't go with the crowd
Don't do what they all do.
Be honest with yourself
And be like you.

ONE: Do you love lots of food? [*Plate*] Yum yum!

TWO: Do you hate slimy snakes? [*Snake*] Sss sss!

ONE: D'you think that you're perfect? [*Halo*] Ping!

TWO: Do you drink milk shakes? [*Straw*] Slurr rrp!

BOTH: [*As before*]
Don't go with the crowd
Don't do what they all do.
Be honest with yourself
And be like you.

ONE: Hang on, what do you mean, 'be like you'?

TWO: Not me, you.

ONE: You?

TWO: No, you.

ONE: You who? [*Laughs*] Yoo hoo!

TWO: That's right. [*Points to him*] You!

ONE: And you. [*Points to her*]

BOTH: [*pointing to audience*] And you!

TWO: I was thinking, what's the point of following everyone else? Listen, don't be like Fred. [ONE *becomes Fred.*]
Fred was a bloke who couldn't take a joke,
In fact he was very mean.
His mother used to shout 'Take your wellies out!
That floor was nice and clean!'
But Fred said

ONE: Do it yourself!

TWO: 'Cos that's what he thought all his other friends

142

said.

ONE: I'm gonna do me homework.

TWO: But he sat on his bed, put his Walkman on, [ONE *uses beads.*]

Turned up the volume 'til his mum's voice was gone

And patted himself on the back [ONE *has a lot of trouble patting his back.*] That'll do, thank you. You see Fred told lies and shouted at his mum just because he thought everyone else did.

ONE: Oh, I see...

TWO: We often do things just because it's a craze.

ONE: I know what you mean. [*During this section* ONE *squeezes the beads to stick them onto the parts of his face as indicated.*]

TWO: We all want to look good.

ONE: [*bead to middle of forehead*] Of course.

TWO: Say the right things.

ONE: [*to bottom lip*] Right.

TWO: Wear the right clothes.

ONE: [*to one cheek*] Yeah.

TWO: Even sing like a pop star sings.

ONE: [*to other cheek, singing*] All right!

TWO: Make lots of friends.

ONE: [*to one jowl*] You bet.

TWO: Have a lot of fun.

ONE: [*to other jowl*] Whoopee!

TWO: Get what you want.

ONE: [*to one side under the chin*] Why not?

TWO: Treat yourself as number one!

ONE: [*to other side under chin*] Da daa!

TWO: And you end up...looking silly!

ONE: You're not kidding!

TWO: But... [*pause*]

ONE: Hurry up, this is agony!

TWO: [*the beads are pulled off to the rhythm indicated.*] Don't go with the crowd [ONE *pulls off jowl beads to two beats and drops them on the floor.*]

Don't do what they all do [*Chin beads, two beats, to the floor*]
Be honest with yourself [*Cheeks, two beats, floor*]
And be like you! [*Forehead and lip, one beat*]

ONE: Ooh, that's better. I've heard of body-popping but this is ridiculous.
[*Throws remaining beads over his shoulders*]

TWO: Listen to some of the things people say: [*They stand back to back, turning head to audience as each speaks.*]

ONE: I ignore my mum and dad

TWO: 'Cos everyone else does.

ONE: I read the stars

TWO: 'Cos everyone else does.

ONE: I follow the trends

TWO: 'Cos everyone else does.

ONE: I follow Jesus...

TWO: [*about to speak. Pause*]...Not everyone does that, do they? [*They look at each other.*]

BOTH: [*realising*] Don't go with the crowd!
Don't go with the crowd
Don't do what they all do.
Be honest with yourself
And be like you!
Dan Daddla daadaa...

TWO: Come on, then!

ONE: We're just popping off! [BOTH *grimace at joke as they join up remaining beads as a rope with* TWO *leading* ONE *off.*]

BOTH: See ya!

144

27. Mulled Wine

Giving a Hand
A meditation by Steve Stickley

The relationship between the physical and spiritual is greatly ignored in our culture. We readily accept without question that when we pray we generally shut our eyelids, we get on to our feet to sing hymns, and may even deprive our stomachs of food as an act of sacrifice. Anything a little more quirky, such as sprawling ourselves prostrate on the floor to pray, is regarded with a great deal of suspicion. (Who knows, maybe we don't do it because it is incompatible with wearing Sunday best.)

For those interested in stimulating a fresh response to worship, the whole area of body-use is ripe for exploration. Giving a Hand provides a simple opportunity to get you started. It is written in script form and should be learnt, although your own style and idiom should be adopted as it is vital that you sound natural and at ease with the idea.

[*Worshippers should be seated. The* LEADER *should encourage them to put down books, handbags, etc, and he or she should join in with every stage throughout the meditation. The pace is gentle and steady.*]

LEADER: Place your hands, palms up, on your lap. Concentrate on your own hands and listen carefully. Look at your hands: resting, open

'The relationship between the
physical and spiritual is greatly
ignored'

on your lap. Gently close them to form two fists...gently. These hands represent your life. Keep looking at them: your life as it once was, closed up, turned away from God. Gently squeeze your hands closed: your life rebelling against God, closed in on itself. Squeeze a bit more. Look carefully at these two fists, the knuckles turning white with the stress. Squeeze a bit more. [*Pause*] This life, locked away...imprisoned...closed in on itself. Squeeze harder. A life of darkness...shut away. This is the only way your life knows, to close itself off. Self-preservation. Fear. Keep squeezing. [*Pause*] The stress is increasing. Someone tells you that Jesus can set you free, but you don't like the sound of that, so you squeeze even harder. [*Slowly building the tension*] You will never open up. No one can tell you what to do. Squeeze harder. You're locked away, you always have been, why change now? Squeeze harder still. Why can't they just leave you alone? Go away, God! Squeeze as hard as you can. [*Pause. Slowly soften the tone.*] But you can't fight forever. Set me free, Lord Jesus. And slowly, *very* slowly, allow your fists to unfold...slowly...slower still...Jesus takes away the stress, opens up your life and sets you free. Keep unfolding *very* slowly. As your life opens, the darkness has gone. And slowly, clumsily your fingers open up...like something newly born. [*Pause*] Until at last your hands are fully open. A life rescued from destruction and pain. Look carefully, there may even be nail marks in your palms. Jesus has set you free. [*Pause, breaking the atmosphere*] OK, give your hands a quick shake and wriggle. Good. Right, now, for this last part we look at our hands again, this new life Christ has given us. [*Encourage the participants to recommence the meditation as seems appropriate*.] This time as we place our hands on our laps as before, I want you to think of all the things these hands are good at. Maybe they are good at cooking, gardening, comforting, or encouraging. [*Pause*] Perhaps they're good at driving, writing or simply waving. Think of all the things your hands can do. [*Pause*] Look at any rings you may be wearing. Why are they there? Do they have any significance? [*Pause*] These are your hands, Like an open book, all about you. [*Pause*] In a moment we are going to offer our hands, our lives, to God. We'll say, 'Take my hands and let them move at the impulse of your love,' as we give our hands to the Lord. [*Repeat the response if you think the participants are unfamiliar with it*.] Now we lift our hands with our palms facing upwards and say together, 'Take my hands and let them move, at the impulse of your love.' And as we hold our hands there, giving them to the Lord, we offer our lives for him to use. As we open our hands, our lives to give to God...so too, are we ready to receive. [*Pause*] Amen.

(NB: *This should not be attempted involving sufferers from arthritis.*)

TABLE D'HÔTE

28. Three course dinner

*Preaching and drama have in general maintained an
uneasy truce in church life. There has been the occasional
outbreak of hostilities, when drama has accused preaching
of defending its own prominence in the church out of self-
interest, and of being blind to the possibilities of drama in
the modern world; to which preaching has returned fire
denouncing drama as having sold out to the 'spirit of the
age' or the latest trends, and of ignoring the Bible's
emphasis on the primacy of the 'preached word'.*

*This feast of ideas for adults at an evening service goes a
long way to offer a pragmatic reconciliation. Close liaison
with the minister or preacher is vital for its success. The
sermon notes are intended as a useful guide to show the
thought process involved, and the person preaching must
obviously use them as he or she thinks fit.* **Vee ask Ze
Qvestions** *should simply begin without introduction, the
minister or preacher should pick up immediately from its
end, and* **'Ark at him** *. . . should interrupt the sermon at the
point indicated.*

German sausage

Vee Ask Ze Qvestions
by Alan MacDonald

Characters:　BAMFORTH—male
　　　　　　　INTERROGATOR—female

[*A chair centre stage in which sits* BAMFORTH. *He wears a white shirt, unbuttoned at the neck, a loosened tie and dark trousers. His hair is tousled and his face perspiring. A standard lamp shines directly into his eyes. Standing behind him is the* INTERROGATOR. *She wears a long raincoat, black gloves, heavy-framed glasses. The general appearance is of an SS interrogator as familiar from old war films.*]

INTERROGATOR:　[*in a heavy German accent*] I will ask you the question again. What do you know about Operation Flood?

BAMFORTH:　[*keeping a British stiff upper lip*] Under the terms of the Keswick Convention I am only required to tell you my name, rank and favourite Bible verse.

INTERROGATOR:　I warn you it is not wise to play the hero. For the last time, what *is* Operation Flood?

BAMFORTH:　Harry Bamforth, soldier of Christ, rejoice in the Lord always...

INTERROGATOR:　So...

BAMFORTH:　And again I say rejoice.

INTERROGATOR:　Bamforth. We have ways of making you talk. [*She fetches a cassette player from upstage.*]

BAMFORTH:　Hah! You think you can frighten me with that old line from British war films. What's that?

INTERROGATOR:　Music to interrogate by. Max Bygraves' Favourite Melodies, volume one. We

	have all four volumes. [*She switches the music on.*]
BAMFORTH:	[*holding out for as long as he can*] All right! All right, I'll talk. [*She switches off.*]
INTERROGATOR:	Good. So now we can get down to business. What was Operation Flood?
BAMFORTH:	A plan to destroy the entire human race by means of deluge covering the earth's surface. Code named... Operation Flood.
INTERROGATOR:	And was this plan ever carried out?
BAMFORTH:	Of course.
INTERROGATOR:	Successfully?
BAMFORTH:	Yes.
INTERROGATOR:	How do you know this?
BAMFORTH:	It's in the Bible.
INTERROGATOR:	Of course. The Bible. Genesis...
BAMFORTH:	Six to eight, and some of chapter nine.
INTERROGATOR:	Which you regard as a reliable historical record.
BAMFORTH:	I don't think there's much doubt about that. God knows what he's talking about.
INTERROGATOR:	[*darkly*] The question is, Bamforth—do you? [*Pause. Moving in*] When did this flood take place?
BAMFORTH:	Oh, a long time ago.
INTERROGATOR:	A long time ago?
BAMFORTH:	Near the beginning of time.
INTERROGATOR:	So in the beginning, God made the world, then soon afterwards he decided he'd made a mistake.
BAMFORTH:	Not a mistake. Men destroyed, they were sinful.
INTERROGATOR:	Men are always sinful.
BAMFORTH:	Yes, but in those days they were... very sinful.

INTERROGATOR:	So God decided to kill them all.
BAMFORTH:	Except Noah.
INTERROGATOR:	Except Noah, of course. God looks down from heaven then and sees mankind being very sinful, so he prepares 'Operation Flood'.
BAMFORTH:	Yes. Rain for forty days and nights. Like six weeks' holiday in Skegness. [*Laughs feebly.*]
INTERROGATOR:	And how old does your Bible say Noah was at this point?
BAMFORTH:	Oh, pretty old, into his seventies I expect.
INTERROGATOR:	Six hundred years old, to be precise.
BAMFORTH:	That old?
INTERROGATOR:	Yes, you think that is possible?
BAMFORTH:	Things were different in those days... not so much stress.
INTERROGATOR:	Apart from waiting for the destruction of the world.
BAMFORTH:	Yes.
INTERROGATOR:	Let's talk about the escape plan, shall we? This boat...
BAMFORTH:	The Ark.
INTERROGATOR:	Yes. How big was this Ark?
BAMFORTH:	Pretty big. I mean...[*Extending his arms*]...big.
INTERROGATOR:	Three hundred cubits long, according to your record, that's four hundred and fifty feet long if we assume a cubit as a standard measurement. Twice the size of the *Cutty Sark* or half the size of the *QE2*.
BAMFORTH:	I told you. Big.
INTERROGATOR:	It would have to be, wouldn't it?
BAMFORTH:	I don't follow.
INTERROGATOR:	How many species are there in the animal kingdom, Bamforth?

BAMFORTH: Gosh, thousands.

INTERROGATOR: At least a million. Even if we allow
                that these have descended from a
                smaller number of species, we are left
                with a conservative estimate of a
                hundred thousand. So that means
                there must have been space for over
                two hundred thousand animals on this
                boat.

BAMFORTH: Some were tiny, like hamsters.

INTERROGATOR: And what about the giraffes, the
                hippopotamus, the elephants?

BAMFORTH: They were given more space.

INTERROGATOR: So once you've packed in these two
                hundred thousand animals and eight
                homo sapiens, where do you store
                enough food for a year?

BAMFORTH: A year?

INTERROGATOR: The flood lasted a year.

BAMFORTH: [*getting flustered*] I don't know. In the
                hold.

INTERROGATOR: And then animals start breeding.

BAMFORTH: I suppose so.

INTERROGATOR: And there's another problem.

BAMFORTH: Vot?...er, What?

INTERROGATOR: Natural by-products.

BAMFORTH: [*pause*] Ah.

INTERROGATOR: Naturally you have an answer for all
                these minor problems?

BAMFORTH: Naturally. [*Thinks*] Nothing is impos-
                sible for God.

INTERROGATOR: The profundity of your faith is stag-
                gering.

BAMFORTH: Thankyou.

INTERROGATOR: The polar bear, he was on the Ark?

BAMFORTH: Of course, or his original ancestor.

INTERROGATOR: How did he get there?

BAMFORTH: What do you mean, 'How did he get

	there?' He walked.
INTERROGATOR:	Like Jesus.
BAMFORTH:	Pardon?
INTERROGATOR:	Like Jesus. He had to come from the Arctic Circle to the Plains of Mesopotamia. so naturally he must have walked upon the water to cross the Atlantic.
BAMFORTH:	He could have swum.
INTERROGATOR:	A few thousand miles, stopping off at the Mediterranean for an ice cream to make him feel at home?
BAMFORTH:	Well, I don't know! I'm not God, am I?
INTERROGATOR:	No, thankfully, you're not. But supposing you were for a minute, why do you create a people for your own pleasure and then drown almost every one of them when you are supposed to be a God of love? [*Moving menacingly closer*] Isn't that rather sadistic?
BAMFORTH:	Not if they disobeyed me. If they were a bunch of criminals and failures. Anyone who's a sinner deserves to die, don't they?
INTERROGATOR:	[*regarding him thoughtfully*] As you say. [*A long pause. Then she drops her German accent.*] That will be all, thankyou, Mr Bamforth. [*She turns off the lamp. He stands up. She takes off her coat, revealing a floral dress and a large wooden cross around her neck.*] I've enjoyed our little interview, but having discussed your application with the bishop and now talking to you myself, I'm afraid to say that we don't feel that we can recommend you

155

for ordination into the Church of
England.
[*She offers her hand.*]

Sunday Roast

Sermon notes: Noah's flood

For about fifteen minutes the preacher looks at the
Genesis 6 and 7 story as an example of God's judgement:
1. Dealing with objections to the concept of God's
punishment of evil.
2. Showing how the evil in the world has its origins
within each of us and that therefore we are each liable
to God's judgement.
3. Reading Matthew 24:7–42 to show how the New
Testament uses Noah's flood as a picture of the final
judgement which will take place when Jesus returns to
earth. (The interruption occurs here.)

Apocalypse Surprise

'Ark at him...
by Steve Stickley

[A *and* B *move out from congregation laughing raucously
with drinks in hand.* A *has a cocktail with attendant
decorations,* B *has what looks like a goatskin wine bag and
could wear biblical headdress. Both are merry and talkative
but not drunk. They stand casually side by side, each never
acknowledging the other. They talk to an imagined friend.*]

A,B: You'd never get *him* along to a party like this...not
       in a million years. Cheers! [*They each drink.* B *has
       slight problems with the bag.*]

B: No, he's too obsessed with that blinkin' boat he's

building. Do you know, he reckons this desert'll be flooded? No joke. [*Laughs and attempts to drink again.*]

A: No, he's got this thing about Jesus making a sort of universal global comeback all over the world, at the same time! No kiddin'. That's fundamentalism for you... not much *fun* being *mental*! [*Laughs and drinks again.* B *has meanwhile squeezed a drop out.*]

A,B: Ahh! That's good stuff that.

A: Sainsburys do a good selection don't they?

B: Did you tread it yourself?

A: Hmm... je ne sais quoi...

B: [*sniffing*] Piquant. [A *drinks again.*] No... Noah must have a screw loose, I mean, you know what he's going to do don't you, he's putting animals in there as well. Yeah! A bloomin' zoo, in a boat, in the desert, no water. [*Laughs and then attempts the wine bag again.*]

A: Naa... that preacher bloke's gotta be bonkers, cranky. I mean, you know these preacher-types don't you? Earthquakes, rolling clouds, cosmic trumpets, bodies floating up into the sky... it's a load of old Walt Disney... [*Shakes his head knowingly.*]

B: Never seen such folly.

A: He's off his trolley.

A,B: What a wally. [*Both drink.*]

A: Is this the Eurythmics? Yeah, I like this one...

B: She's really goin' it on that psaltery isn't she?

A: Sad, really, he's so out of touch. I mean he knows as much about real life as the Archbishop of Canterbury knows about body popping.

B: It's tragic, really. Do you know he never ever has any orgies, drunken revelries, idol worship or baby sacrifices? He hasn't lived! Not liberated. [*Shakes head sadly.*]

A: Talk about Christians being old-fashioned, he even looks like he's just come out of the ark.

B: You've got to move with the times, after all ... [*Both shake their heads and sup a little more.*]

A: He reckons this second coming thing will alter history on a global scale, just like that! [*He clicks fingers.*]

B: He reckons this flood will wipe out life as we know it, just like that! [*Tries to click his fingers, fails. Tries other hand, fails.*] Anyway, did you hear him the other day? 'Believe me, it's going to happen. Trust me, you'll be safe!' Tut!

A: [*impersonating the preacher for all he is worth.*] 'Believe in Jesus, he's coming back. Trust him, you'll be saved!' Tut!

A,B: I wasn't born yesterday, you know. [*A finishes drink. B wrings out the bag.*] Oh, well, it takes all sorts. [*Both look around at the party briefly. A thought suddenly occurs to them.*] He reckons it's God's judgement, y'know. [*They snigger.*]

A: Talk about Victorian values ...

B: These new-fangled ideas ...

A,B: Well, I'll trust my own judgement, thank you very much. [*Pause.*]

B: Looks a bit like rain ... [*A is absentmindedly fiddling with his cocktail umbrella. Pause.*]

If you feel it necessary for any further comment to follow this, it should be concise and to the point ... no more than one minute at the most. Perhaps a response in prayer may be appropriate.

THE
END